D1165432

WHEN SHEA
WAS HOME

WHEN SHEA WAS HOME

THE STORY OF THE 1975 METS, YANKEES, GIANTS, AND JETS

BRETT TOPEL

Sports Publishing books may be purchased in bulk at special discounts for sales promotion, corporate gifts, fund-raising, or educational purposes. Special editions can also be created to specifications. For details, contact the Special Sales Department, Sports Publishing, 307 West 36th Street, 11th Floor, New York, NY 10018 or sportspubbooks@ skyhorsepublishing.com.

Sports Publishing® is a registered trademark of Skyhorse Publishing, Inc.®, a Delaware corporation.

Visit our website at www.sportspubbooks.com.

10 9 8 7 6 5 4 3 2 1

Library of Congress Cataloging-in-Publication Data is available on file.

Cover design by Tom Lau
Cover photos credits National Baseball Hall of Fame Library (top) and AP Images (bottom)

ISBN: 978-1-61321-870-9
Ebook ISBN: 978-1-61321-871-6
Printed in the United States of America

Dedicated to my children,
Oliver and Lily

Contents

Preface   ix

Chapter 1:   The Birth of a Crazy Season   1

Chapter 2:   The Queens Bombers   17

Chapter 3:   Big Shea   45

Chapter 4:   Meet the Mets   67

Chapter 5:   New York State of Mind   95

Chapter 6:   When Baseball Ended, and the Football Season Began   115

Chapter 7:   The Aftermath of 1975   133

Acknowledgments   159

Sources   161

Index   165

Preface

I ALWAYS WANTED TO WRITE a book about Shea Stadium, and in the summer of 2012, I finally came up with an angle I thought would work well. I just had to bounce it off my usual baseball focus group—my dad.

That week, the two of us attended the Mets-Phillies game at Citi Field. For this particular game, I purchased tickets for us in Section 125, Row D—five rows off the field, well beyond the infield cutout and down the third-base line. I normally wouldn't have selected these seats, as I have always agreed with my dad's philosophy that it's better to be "up than out," meaning that we prefer seats higher up in the stadium, but more toward home plate. For whatever reason, that night I chose those seats.

We arrived at the stadium early—as we always do—usually to talk and, more importantly, to eat. I started talking about the idea I had for a book, or a magazine article, or something, involving the Mets, Yankees, Jets, and Giants all sharing Shea Stadium in 1975. My dad loved the idea and encouraged me to pursue it. I explained to him that the only way to really get started was to somehow get in touch with Pete Flynn, who had been the Mets' head groundskeeper at Shea Stadium and is now retired.

I decided I was going to ask one of the current groundskeepers if they knew how I could get in touch with Flynn. I made my way down toward the field and called out to one of the groundskeepers, who was working on the field before the game. He informed me that I needed to speak with his boss, Bill, who was the head groundskeeper. A few minutes later, Bill Deacon walked over and asked how he could help me. I explained what I wanted and he told me that Pete sometimes was at games, and if I gave him my phone number, he or someone else would pass it along to Pete. I told him that would be great.

Just then, he looked toward the tunnel where the groundskeepers entered the field and gestured for me to turn around. "Right over there," he said. "Pete, he is right over there," motioning over my shoulder.

I turned around and there—standing next to the railing of my section—was, in fact, Pete Flynn. I think—or hope—I thanked Bill Deacon. I remember walking toward Flynn, trying to figure out in five seconds how I was going to explain to him who I was, and what I wanted to do. "Mr. Flynn," I said, as he turned to look at me, "my name is Brett Topel and I am an author who is thinking about writing a book about the 1975 season at Shea." Pete Flynn glanced away from me, stared toward the infield, and uttered the words that convinced me that I *had* to write this book. In a quiet, trailing Irish brogue, he said . . . "Ahh, that season be the death of me."

I asked him if I could have his contact information and give him a call the next day to talk about the 1975 season. He agreed. I walked back to where my dad was sitting and told him what had transpired. He just laughed. I laughed too, as it was a surreal and unexpected outcome. For that one game, and for this one book, "out" was definitely better than "up."

· · · ·

While I was able to interview Pete Flynn the very next day, it took nearly three more years until the book became a reality. Then, one week after signing a contract to write *When Shea Was Home* for Skyhorse Publishing, a second surreal moment took place that helped shape my writing journey.

When I was in college, I fell in love with a bunch of songs by a singer named Midge Ure. He had been the lead singer of a band called Ultravox and had written the charity song, *Do They Know It's Christmas?*, before releasing a couple of solo albums in the late 1980s and early 1990s. However, few people I know were familiar with Midge Ure.

Then, in February of 2015, I saw that Midge was scheduled to perform an acoustic show at a small Long Island restaurant, not far from my home. I asked my wife if she would like to go and she begrudgingly agreed. After all, it had been more than twenty years since I had forced her to listen to a Midge Ure song and I figured one night wouldn't kill her. We could celebrate my book deal with a night out.

In all honesty, though, I wasn't really thinking about the book on the night of the concert; I was really just looking forward to hearing Midge Ure perform. It was a small, crowded restaurant and people were forced to share tables. After finishing our dinner, just as the show was about to start, another couple was directed toward our table. I wasn't thrilled, but I also wasn't going to make an issue out of it. Then I heard my wife say, "Oh, my God, look who it is." It turns out that the people who were seated with us—somehow—were my daughter's former pre-school teacher, Mrs. Ross, and her husband.

Mrs. Ross introduced me to her husband, Larry, and then said to me, "Hey, you're really into sports, right?" I nodded. She then uttered the words that would blow me away and change my night—and really, in many ways, my future. "You know, Larry's first cousin is Marty Appel, who used to work for the Yankees."

Huh?[1]

I turned to Larry Ross and said, "Are you serious?" He said, "Absolutely."

---

[1] Side note: In the days since signing the book deal, I had been making a list of people that I wanted to interview for this book. I already had some contact with former Mets, but I needed someone all-knowing about the Yankees. That's when I stumbled upon Marty Appel's outstanding book, *Pinstripe Pride*. That was the guy!

I then went on to tell to him about the book I was writing and how Marty Appel was someone that I had been trying to get in touch with, etc. He could have just nodded and said, "Wow, small world." Instead, he snapped into superhero mode, took out his phone, and sent an email to Marty, with me cc'd, introducing the two of us. Two days later, I was having a terrific telephone interview with Marty Appel, who could not have been more accommodating.

Meeting Pete Flynn and Larry Ross in the ways that I did were something that I could neither plan nor predict. Yet, they are two of the most significant moments of my journey.

Midge Ure really only had one hit in the United States, which came out in 1988, and was called *Dear God*. The opening lines were:

Dear God, is there somebody out there?
Is there someone to hear my prayer?
I'm a simple man with simple words to say.

CHAPTER 1

The Birth of a Crazy Season

As NEW YORKERS AWOKE ON Monday, December 22, 1975, there was a light, serene snow falling. There was a chill in the air, and by the end of the day just about two inches of precipitation would blanket the New York City metropolitan area. Just days before Christmas, the first measurable snow of the winter provided a thin coating for the infield dirt—and outfield dirt—of the large, horseshoe-shaped stadium set on the edge of Flushing Bay. There was no grass left in the stadium for the snow to cover.

Later that evening, 60 percent of televisions in the United States tuned in to watch the birth of Joey Stivic, the first grandchild of Edith and Archie Bunker, fictionally set at 704 Hauser Street, just a few miles from that big stadium.

One day earlier, on December 21, 1975, Shea Stadium had been hardly packed, with 37,279 fans—less than half of its capacity for football. The New York Jets were playing out the string of a 3-11 campaign with a 31-21 loss to the Super Bowl–bound Dallas Cowboys. The final loss of the season was good enough for the Jets to finish in a tie for last place in the Eastern Division of the American Football Conference.

The loss was much more bitter than bittersweet for the Jets, who watched their blossoming running back, John Riggins, gain more than

100 yards for the fifth consecutive game. His 121 hard-earned yards against Dallas put him over the 1,000-yard mark, as Riggins finished the 1975 season with a total of 1,005 rushing yards. He became the first player in New York Jets history to reach that milestone and was named the team's Most Valuable Player. He would never play for the Jets again.

Riggins's rushing accomplishment notwithstanding, to say that Shea Stadium went out with a whimper in 1975 is an understatement—with all due respect to T. S. Eliot.

However, that final game was the final act of eight months of non-stop, wall-to-wall, game-to-game, season-to-season, sport-to-sport action at Shea Stadium.

You see, if you wanted to take in a home game for the New York Mets, or the New York Yankees, or the New York Jets, or the New York Giants that year, then you would need to make the trip to Shea Stadium. That was the one and only stadium open for business in 1975—for more than 175 games, with well over 3.7 million fans, and far too many hot dogs to count. Victories, however—for all four teams—were much harder to come by.

If 1975 wasn't the most successful season in New York (and it wasn't), then it was certainly one of the oddest—not just for the events that happened inside the stadium, but also for the events within the city that owned the stadium.

As the baseball season had turned into the football season, the president of the United States was New York City's archenemy. The infamous October 30 cover of the New York *Daily News* carried the bold headline: "Ford to City: Drop Dead." The fact that President Gerald Ford never actually uttered those words is often forgotten. However, the truth was, New York City was in a horrific economic crisis and the nation's leadership initially had no interest in providing any help. That changed when President Ford announced that he would relent and provide a federal rescue. New York City would indeed survive 1975—much like Shea Stadium would.

• • • •

"We are going to see this through," New York City mayor Robert Wagner proudly announced on April 12, 1960. "We couldn't turn back now if we wanted to."

The original concept of a new stadium being built in Queens dated back as far as 1940. However, by the mid to late 1950s, the goal of building the stadium was to keep the Brooklyn Dodgers in New York. Dodgers owner Walter O'Malley insisted that if he was going to consider keeping his team in New York City, he needed a brand-new stadium in Brooklyn. Urban planner and architect Robert Moses didn't really seem to care what O'Malley wanted. He offered to build O'Malley's team a new, modern stadium in Queens—and only in Queens. The Dodgers could take it or leave it. O'Malley left it, and convinced his biggest rival—the crosstown New York Giants baseball club—to follow his team's lead and move to California following the 1957 season.

Moses was unfazed. He was often unfazed. The man who was obsessed with taking people out of the city and into the suburbs continued on with his plan to have a giant, multi-sport stadium constructed on the site of what had been—and what would once again be—the World's Fair Grounds in Flushing Meadow Park. Moses was the president of the upcoming 1964 World's Fair and wanted a centerpiece. According to the 1964 World's Fair Guide Book, "Long after the Fair is gone, Shea Stadium will remain as the ultimate in modern sports arenas." Of course, Queens is a borough of New York City and not technically the suburbs. However, it was open land and it was land that Moses was going to paint with his broad brush.

The architectural firm of Praeger-Kavanaugh-Waterbury was selected to design what would become the second stadium in the nation capable of hosting both baseball and football games. However, unlike D.C. Stadium in Washington, Shea would be the first major league stadium to utilize two sets of moveable stands to allow for changes in seating capacity for baseball and football. This was made possible via the use of two motor-operated sections of the seats that moved on underground-railroad tracks. For baseball seating, the seats between first base and home plate and between third base and home plate were able to shift. For football seating, the left-field stands were able to move clockwise to face center field and the right-field stands moved counterclockwise toward center field, creating seats that were parallel to the sidelines.

The design of Shea also marked the first time that a stadium would be built without the use of support beams in between each level of the building, allowing fans superior sight lines.

Moses was confident that it would be a state-of-the-art playing facility, with high-tech advancements such as the first-of-its-kind electronic scoreboard, which would stand a hulking eighty-six feet high by one-hundred-seventy-five feet wide. Moses also wanted to make sure that—unlike Ebbets Field in Brooklyn and the Polo Grounds in Manhattan—there would plenty of large, clean restrooms. In fact, Shea Stadium was designed to include fifty-four public restrooms, twenty-seven for men and twenty-seven for women.

However, what Moses bragged loudest about was that it would be the most accessible stadium the area had ever experienced. That was, at his core, what Moses was all about—building roads and highways and designing suburban infrastructure. His new stadium in Queens would be a perfect fit at the perfect time.

On October 28, 1961, ground was broken.

At Mayor Wagner's urging and with the backing of other prominent civic leaders, the new stadium—which was originally going to be called Flushing Meadows Stadium—was named for William A. Shea, a New York City–based attorney who was instrumental in bringing National League baseball back to New York in the form of the expansion New York Mets.

"For the christening ceremony, Mr. Shea filled two empty champagne bottles with water—one from the Harlem River, near the old Polo Grounds, and the other from the Gowanus Canal in Brooklyn. Though you could not see the canal from Ebbets Field, he explained, you could always smell it," David Margolick wrote in the *New York Times*.

When the Mets held their first-ever Opening Day in April of 1964—after two bitter winters and no less than seventeen labor strikes had delayed its opening—Shea Stadium's electronic scoreboard spelled out the phrase: "Isn't this the most beautiful stadium in the world." As author W. M. Akers wrote, "The message had no question mark, because the city knew the answer had to be yes."

• • • •

Shea's metamorphosis into the only game in town truly began when the New York Yankees played their final game of the 1973 season at Yankee Stadium on September 30; fans walked out of the big ballpark in the Bronx carrying seats home with them as souvenirs. The days of charging hundreds and even thousands of dollars for pieces of old stadiums was still more than three decades away. For the Yankees, having fans take those seats just meant that there was less for the organization to have hauled away. The seats that remained in the ballpark were offered to season ticket holders, and then went on sale for $5.75 each at Korvette's Department Store as part of a promotion with Winston cigarettes. In comparison, when Shea Stadium was torn down in 2008, a pair of seats sold for $869.

Some of the other artifacts from Yankee Stadium were purchased by former players who wanted to always have a piece of the House That Ruth Built. Stan Musial purchased some of the bleacher seats for his restaurant in St. Louis, and former Yankees Whitey Ford and Yogi Berra were among those who purchased some of the box seats for themselves.

Other than the seats, the majority of the innards of Yankee Stadium were sold to a collector by the name of Bert Sugar, who paid the Yankees for the rights to take what he wished. Whatever Sugar didn't take was simply given to Cleveland's Cuyahoga Wrecking Company, which sold off to collectors and fans. Some of those items included turnstiles for $100 each and the "In" sign from a men's bathroom, which was priced at $3.

It was on this final day of the home season in the Bronx—an unremarkable 8-5 victory by the Detroit Tigers over the Yankees —that would put a temporary end to Yankee Stadium. The plan was under way.

The Yankees would be spending the 1974 and 1975 seasons sharing Shea with the Mets and Jets—an idea that had been roundly criticized years earlier by M. Donald Grant, the chairman of the Mets board.

"Two baseball clubs have never worked well in the same stadium," Grant told the *New York Times* in 1971. "One club always suffers. I don't think (Yankees President) Michael Burke wants to have his team in Shea Stadium any more than we want ours in Yankee Stadium. Would you like to give a very important party in my house?"

Things changed, however, when New York City purchased Yankee Stadium the following year. New York City Mayor John Lindsay and the Yankees' new ownership—led by Cleveland-based shipbuilder George Steinbrenner—announced that Yankee Stadium would undergo an extensive two-year renovation. New York City also owned Shea Stadium, which gave the Mets little choice but to allow their American League counterparts from the Bronx to share their turf—literally.

By the start of the 1974 baseball season, the "party" that Grant had poked fun about a few years earlier began. The Mets, Yankees, and Jets all called Shea Stadium home.

"It really, really was surreal and felt more than just a little uncomfortable to my eyes to see the Yankees logo hung over the Mets logo on top of the big scoreboard in right-center field," said Howie Rose, the foremost authority on Mets' history, who has been a Mets broadcaster in one capacity or another for nearly thirty years. "That Mets logo was actually the [front] of what was originally a video screen that seemed to work once every five years or so. Obviously, the Yankees had to do something to personalize the ballpark when they were there, and that was really the extent of it. I have to tell you, it was more than a little disconcerting to this Mets fan. The Yankees belonged in the Bronx, the Mets belonged in Queens, and never the 'tween shall meet, except perhaps in the World Series."

Rose, who was a Queens College student in 1974, was still a year away from getting a job as a staff member for Sports Phone—which gave fans in-progress sports delivered on tape by young and aspiring sportscasters. He was hired as the weekend night announcer on the

The hulking scoreboard in right-center field looked strange with the Yankees logo perched on top. *Photo courtesy of Larry Ross*

recommendation of Marv Albert, who knew Rose as the one-time president of his fan club.

"I was right on that precipice of being a full-time media member, but I wasn't yet," Rose said. "So most of the time—because Shea Stadium was so close to where I lived—it was easy for me to get in my car and shoot over there. There were a lot of times where my friends and I went to games there and while obviously the Mets were our priority, if there was a Yankees game and I had a chance to go see it, sure we went. It was fun, but it was different. And I would say it was more than a little uncomfortably different. The Yankees were the Bronx—they didn't belong there. They looked and felt very out of place."

For the Mets players themselves, sharing the stadium was not really a big deal.

"I don't think it really meant anything to us, because we were always on the road when they were playing there," said Ed Kranepool, who in 1974 was already a twelve-year veteran at the age of twenty-nine. "We never crossed paths. I was a Yankee fan growing up, so it really didn't make a difference to me. Growing up, there were just the Yankees, Dodgers, and Giants until I graduated high school and went to the Mets."

The Mets—only one year removed from a World Series appearance—slipped to fifth place with just 71 wins in 1974. One of the few memorable games of the year was a 25-inning loss to the St. Louis Cardinals. Following a terrific 1973 season during which he led his team to the pennant, ace Tom Seaver managed just twelve victories and twelve losses in '74. The Mets, led by manager Yogi Berra, ranked at the bottom, or near the bottom, of almost every offensive category. As a team, the Mets had a batting average of just .235—second to last in the National League. Only the San Diego Padres, who lost more than 100 games in 1974, had a lower average than the Mets.

The cross-stadium rival Yankees, on the other hand, seemed to acclimate well to their new surroundings. It was the first time that the Yankees had played their home games outside of Yankee Stadium since 1922, and they played very well, finishing the 1974 campaign with eighty-nine victories. Setting up shop in the New York Jets clubhouse, the Yankees made a run at the division, finishing just two games behind the American League East Champion Boston Red Sox. They had several promising young players and a new manager in Bill Virdon. However, their highest-paid player was less than enthusiastic about his new home.

Bobby Murcer—coming off of a 22-home run campaign at Yankee Stadium in 1973—struggled mightily at Shea Stadium. The right-field fence was nearly 40 feet deeper at Shea than it was at Yankee Stadium and Murcer didn't hit a single home run at home in 1974 until September 21. He finished the season with just one other homer at Shea and only ten in total for the season. He was traded to the San Francisco Giants a month later.

"Bobby Murcer did not like playing at Shea at all," said Marty Appel, who in 1974 was the public relations director of the Yankees.

"He didn't play well there, so it was easy to blame the ballpark, but he really had a big drop off in terms of power numbers."

"He would always complain about how hard it was to play at Shea Stadium with the wind, etcetera," said Kranepool, who was close friends with Murcer. "The fact that the ball didn't carry to right field really hurt him. That ballpark was just not conducive to his game."

By the end of 1974, after falling just short of a division crown, the Yankees' young ownership was ready to make a big move. As the sport would soon learn, when George Steinbrenner went fishing for a top player, he got a top player. Following the 1974 campaign, Steinbrenner didn't want just another top player, though. He wanted *the* top player— no matter what stadium his team was playing in. The result—he caught the biggest Catfish of all.

• • • •

When the baseball season finally came to an end, the 1974 New York Jets took center stage at Shea Stadium. After starting the season at 1-7, the Jets won their final six games of the season to finish with an uplifting 7-7 record.

Joe Namath threw twenty touchdown passes and twenty-two interceptions for the Jets in 1974. Still, it was the first time that Broadway Joe had played a full season since walking out of the Orange Bowl, waving his index finger in the air signifying that he and his Jets were the number-one team in the world. The 1974 Jets season was hardly comparable to the 1969 Super Bowl year, but for Namath things appeared to be moving in the right direction. During the six-game, season-capping winning streak, he threw for eleven touchdowns and only five interceptions. It appeared that the Jets might be on the cusp of something positive.

That feeling would not last long, but at least at the close of 1974 the Jets and their fans had something to cheer about. More than 61,000 fans were on hand to watch the Jets defeat the playoff-bound Buffalo Bills, 20-10, on December 8. That game closed Shea Stadium for the winter.

The 1974 baseball and football seasons at Shea had started and ended with three teams instead of the usual two, and the building and the field seemed no worse for wear.

While Shea was as busy as can be in 1974, an Ivy League stadium just about seventy miles north of Flushing was moving at a much different pace. The New York Giants—playing in New Haven, Connecticut, at the Yale Bowl—were finishing up a 2-12 season, winning exactly zero games at "home." In fact, during the 1973 and 1974 seasons combined, the Giants went just 1-11 in the home of the Yale Bulldogs. The Bulldogs, incidentally, won eight of their nine games that season.

Playing in Connecticut was not part of the Giants' master plan. In 1971, team owner Wellington Mara had announced that for a number of reasons, the team was going to leave Yankee Stadium—their home field since 1956. The Giants' new stadium would be across the Hudson River, in East Rutherford, New Jersey.

"It was a very controversial decision and I remember (my father) faced enormous public criticism for moving out of New York and into New Jersey. The reality was, the Meadowlands was the same distance from Times Square as Yankees Stadium was," said Giants co-owner John Mara. "We had grown tired of being second-class citizens in Yankee Stadium and having to schedule our games around the baseball season. It became increasingly apparent that we weren't going to be able to stay there and that they were going to be renovating the stadium at some point, which was going to end up cutting the capacity, which was a huge problem for us. We were selling out every game and the thought of capacity being reduced was not received very positively."

"More importantly than that, we started to see around that time the construction of football-only stadiums and that was something that we desperately wanted to have for our own. New Jersey came along and made a proposal and we announced in 1971 that we were going to move to New Jersey. I remember (my father) getting criticized aggressively. It was a tough period from that point of view."

By the time the 1974 season came to an end, it seemed very clear that 1976 would most likely be the soonest that the Giants' new stadium in New Jersey would be ready. However, when the Giants were in the market for an interim home in 1973, Wellington Mara made his opinion very clear when he was asked about the possibility of Big Blue playing in Big Shea.

"We've made some provisions for alternate playing sites, but Shea Stadium isn't one of them," Wellington Mara told the *New York Times*. "It's a physical impossibility."

Unfortunately for the Giants, their regular-season experience in Connecticut was dreadful.

"We won one game in our time at the Yale Bowl, so it was definitely not a happy period of time for us," John Mara said.

In fact, after winning just one of their twelve home games at the Yale Bowl, Wellington Mara's attitude about Queens had changed—markedly. In January of 1974, newly elected New York City Mayor Abraham Beame extended a personal invitation to Wellington Mara and the Giants to join the Mets, Yankees, and Jets at Shea Stadium. What once was a "physical impossibility" now was the Giants' very best option for 1975.

"Our players have never accepted (the Yale Bowl) as a home field," he told the *New York Times* following the 1974 season. "If a group of athletes think it's bad, then we're at a competitive disadvantage. . . . I always felt that two football teams couldn't exist at Shea Stadium, but the positive of playing close to home outweighs the negative."

The move to Shea was more out of necessity for the Giants, but the current owner of the team also concedes that his father's decision to return to New York City for that one season might have been a small peace offering to the fans.

"We jumped at the chance to go to Shea Stadium in 1975," John Mara said. "It was really more convenient for our ticket holders to be playing in New York rather than in New Haven, but I think it was partially an olive branch to the New York fans, as well."

Whatever the reason, the decision was well received by the fans—and the New York Giants players.

"It sounds beautiful," Giants safety and ten-year veteran Spider Lockhart told the press after hearing the news that his team would be playing their home games at Shea. "The fact that you're playing in New York is what you're supposed to be doing. I like the idea."

Not everyone was as excited as the Giants players, however.

Following the announcement that the Giants would be joining the Jets at Shea to share the NFL campaign, Jets president and part-owner Philip H. Iselin penned a scathing column in the *New York Times* lamenting what the 1975 season would be like. Iselin was adamant that New York City needed its own football stadium and that no version of a multi-sport stadium would be acceptable.

"The temporary addition of the Giants into Shea Stadium, already overcrowded with our Jets and the baseball Mets and Yankees, simply emphasizes the fact that New York, the great city of the Western World, never has had a football stadium of professional standards," he wrote. "Through the years, all football teams that have played here have been victims of a peculiar priority that has made them orphans. We are unwanted waifs with no contractual advantages in our basic operations. We have back-door status that generally makes it impossible for us to play a home game until the season is nearly one-third over. Comparably, can you imagine the furor that would develop if the Mets or Yankees could not play a home game until sometime around Memorial Day? This is totally unfair."

Iselin was quick to point out that his issues had nothing to do with the Giants themselves, focusing his anger on people higher in the food chain.

"We welcome the Giants," Iselin wrote. "They come to Shea Stadium with our permission—and our blessings. When they are gone, we still will be faced with inequities that have plagued us throughout our history. It is a monstrous problem that cannot be resolved under existing conditions."

Despite the angry ramblings of the Jets president, beginning in April of 1975, the Mets, Yankees, Jets, and Giants played their home campaigns at Shea Stadium. This reality once seemed to be an impossibility, when the Jets and Giants were denied permission to play even a single exhibition game against each other in 1969 at Shea. The Mets had flatly said no when the request was made—something that they could legally do according to their lease with New York City. The Commissioner of Parks for the City of New York, August Heckscher, could not do anything to change the minds of Mets' management. Heckscher acknowledged that he "as well as thousands of New Yorkers would like to see the game played, but confirmed that the existing lease prohibits such a game without the Mets' permission."

However, that was 1969. This was now 1975, and it was official that four teams—175 games on the home schedules, plus the high school and college games and other activities that were planned for Shea Stadium—would play at Shea. The very simple fact was that the destination spot for New York sports fans in 1975 was going to be Shea Stadium.

"Ahh, that season be the death of me," said Pete Flynn, in a hushed Irish brogue, staring straight ahead.

From the day it opened, Flynn was among the men in charge of keeping Shea Stadium's Kentucky bluegrass outfield and dirt infield playable for all games. As a Shea groundskeeper since 1964 Flynn had seen it all—or so he thought. He had been there for the Beatles, for the Amazin' Mets of 1969, and for countless big performances from Tom Seaver to Joe Namath. He was named Shea's head groundskeeper in 1974, just in time for all of the fun. However, 1975 would put Flynn and his staff to the ultimate test.

"It was a nightmare," said Flynn, now retired and deservedly a member of the Major League Baseball Groundskeepers Hall of Fame. "I didn't have a day off for months, and the field never got a day off. By the time the football season was over, there wasn't a blade of grass left in the entire place. That field just wasn't made to be used every day."

The worn field conditions were very evident to members of the Mets, who had gotten used to Shea looking and playing a certain way.

"The field was getting a whole lot of use," Mets pitcher Jon Matlack said. "When we went out on the road, the Yankees would be there, so it was nonstop use. The grounds crew would work overnight and it was a difficult situation to try and keep up with. For me, it seemed like it was dried out, there was less grass, and it generally was not in the same type of shape that it normally was in."

All too often, that was indeed the truth. Dry, hard field conditions in the infield, poor drainage in the outfield, the field never having a day off, and other factors, led to Shea Stadium having many days of sub-par playing conditions—despite the tireless hours and hours Flynn and his staff dedicated to their work.

"Field maintenance wasn't like it was today," Appel said. "Today, all of the fields look really good into September, but back then they would really wear out with everyday use. Shea Stadium was not built on great land anyway; it was pretty swampy."

However, it was not just the land and the wear and tear. In 1975, there was another factor that doomed Shea Stadium's turf.

"People don't even think about this, but players getting off chewing tobacco made field maintenance a lot different," Appel said. "The constant spitting of chewing tobacco back in those days would destroy the field by midseason. The guys, especially outfielders, generally stood in the same place every day and they would spit the tobacco in the same location. That would kill off the grass pretty quickly."

Flynn's staff—aware of the issue—tried their best, at times to little avail.

"We tried to seed in the right and left field areas where the players stood all the time," he said. "We tried to seed that and keep it at least halfway decent."

Field issues, scheduling nightmares, teams sharing clubhouses, and one giant cannonball blast were all ahead for Shea Stadium in 1975. There would be great pitching, Cy Young awards, and catastrophic injuries on the horizon. A future Super Bowl MVP would take the field as a collegiate and Japan's Emperor Hirohito would take in a ballgame.

As the 1975 season was about to start, it would not take long to realize that there would never be another one like it. Never before, and never since, have four professional sports teams shared one facility.

"I don't have too many memories [from 1975], to tell you the truth," Flynn said with something of a chuckle. "Because I try to forget it."

Of course, there was one group that was very enthusiastic about what was to come in 1975.

"It was a bonanza for game-day employees," Appel said. "They made out like bandits."

Growing up just minutes from Shea Stadium not only meant Howie Rose could attend games, but it meant his friends were part of the bonanza.

"I certainly remember the fact that there was a game there every day," said Howie Rose. "I had a couple of friends who were vendors for Harry M. Stevens, which handled the concessions at the time for Mets games and they worked Yankees games too. They absolutely cleaned up, as I recall."

• • • •

In 1975, Robert A. Caro won the Pulitzer Prize in Biography, the Francis Parkman Prize of the Society of American Historians, and the *Washington Monthly* Political Book Award. All of these accolades were for his book entitled *The Power Broker: Robert Moses and the Fall of New York*. Caro's biography of Moses, which has been lauded by *Time* magazine as one of the 100 greatest books of the twentieth century, exposed Moses as a villain, a racist, and a man who displaced hundreds of thousands of New Yorkers to fit his own greedy plans. It portrayed him as a man who did what he pleased, when he pleased, often flying in the face of people who—in reality—sat in positions above him. Quite simply, as Caro put it, "With his power, Robert Moses built himself an empire."

Caro's award-winning "masterpiece of American reporting" finally destroyed Moses's controversial reputation.

Without Robert Moses, however, there never would have been a Shea Stadium.

CHAPTER 2

The Queens Bombers

SITTING IN HIS MISSOURI HOME, forty years after being fired as the manager of the New York Yankees, William Charles "Bill" Virdon was quick to come up with the one word that summed up his experience managing the Yankees in Shea Stadium.

"Different," Virdon recalled.

After all, these were the New York Yankees—perhaps not Ruth and Gehrig, or DiMaggio and Mantle—but it was still a team that had more world championships than any other team in history. They were the Bronx Bombers—yet playing a little less than ten miles from the Bronx.

"It didn't seem right, just because we were the Yankees," Virdon said. "You lived with it, because that was life."

It is one of the most common of Yankees trivia questions: "Name the only Yankees manager to never win a game in Yankee Stadium." Of course, Virdon is also the only Yankees manager to never lose a game at Yankee Stadium, but that detail is usually left out of the trivia books.

In reality, Virdon had real success as the Yankees' skipper, leading his team to an 89–73 record and a second-place finish in 1974. For his efforts, he was named the American League's Manager of the Year.

Virdon was not the Yankees' first choice to be manager in 1974. After longtime Yankees skipper Ralph Houk resigned following the 1973 season, Yankees owner George Steinbrenner wanted very much to hire Dick Williams, the manager of the Oakland Athletics. Williams had just led his Oakland squad to a World Series victory over the New York Mets, and Steinbrenner wanted him badly. It seemed like a perfect fit. Like Houk, Williams had recently resigned his position. He didn't want to work anymore for a meddlesome owner like Oakland's Charles O. Finley. Working for a hands-off owner like George Steinbrenner would be very different—or so he thought. So Williams signed a deal to manage the Yankees. However, there was a problem—Williams was still under contract with the Athletics.

The only way Finley would allow Williams to go across the country and manage Steinbrenner's Yankees was if New York would deliver two top prospects to Oakland. The Yankees refused. The entire mess ended a couple of days later when American League President Joe Cronin voided the contract the Yankees had signed with Williams.

Virdon had just completed a somewhat-successful managerial stint of his own, leading the Pittsburgh Pirates to a National League Eastern Division title in 1972. The following season, his team struggled, and he was let go by the Pirates in September of 1973. He was not out of work for long, as he quickly made an impression on the Yankees in the spring of 1974.

"The transition from Houk to Virdon was a bit of a shock," former Yankee Ron Blomberg wrote in his biography. "Virdon didn't take any crap from anybody. When he had something to get off his chest, he knew how to get the team's attention. He didn't talk much, but when he did, people listened. He placed more restrictions on the team than Ralph did, but regardless of his managerial style, I thought he was an excellent leader."

Virdon had been a player himself, batting .267 during his twelve-year career, eleven of those spent with the Pirates. He was a no-nonsense kind of guy, and his players liked playing for him.

"We called him Popeye because he has such large forearms," Blomberg wrote. "He always wore a short-sleeved shirt to show off what good shape he was in. And he wanted his players in good shape, too. Bill's workouts were tough. He ordered daily baseball running drills that were so demanding that some of the guys complained that it was as if they were in boot camp. Virdon did run a tight ship."

By the time 1975 rolled around, Steinbrenner was getting a little tired of the fact that Virdon was a players' manager. Although he was a leader, he wasn't quite vocal enough for Yankees ownership. So in August of 1975, with the Yankees playing above-.500 ball, Virdon became the first manager to be fired by George Steinbrenner. There would be many others to follow.

• • • •

When the New York Yankees and the City of New York decided that Yankee Stadium was going to go through a major renovation beginning in 1974, they set off a massive chain of events. For one thing, the Yankees would need a place to play. Unluckily for the Yankees, the Mets wanted no part of their crosstown "rivals" sharing their stadium. Luckily for the Yankees, the Mets really had no say in the matter. The City of New York owned both stadiums and made it clear to the Mets that they were going to soon have tenants.

The day before Opening Day of 1974, the Yankees held their final workout at Shea Stadium before the start of the season. Perhaps appropriately, the team took batting practice, long-tossed, and held their entire workout wearing their road gray uniforms.

"It's a little strange for me, because this is my tenth year with the Yankees," said Yankees pitcher Mel Stottlemyre, following the workout. "It almost feels as if I've been traded, but I'm with the same ballplayers."

"We did try to entice some new fans while we were there," said Marty Appel, who was the Yankees Director of Public Relations from 1973 through 1977. "We bought billboards along the Grand Central Parkway and Long Island Expressway saying, 'Hello Queens, the Yankees are Coming.' We didn't do well with attendance and we kind

The Yankees take batting practice prior to the start of a game during the 1975 season. *Photo courtesy of Larry Ross*

Yankees fans never really embraced the idea of traveling to Queens to see their team, but there wasn't a lack of marketing on the team's part.

of said, 'well, it is what it is.' We weren't going to convert Mets fans. I do remember we made an attempt though."

For the Mets players, having the Yankees around was really a non-issue.

"I remember that (the Yankee players) weren't too happy with the dimensions of the park because Shea was a lot bigger than Yankee Stadium," former Mets all-star shortstop Bud Harrelson said. "But I don't remember really even seeing the Yankees at Shea that season. When we were home, they were away, and they used the Jets locker room, so we weren't kicked out of our clubhouse, which was good."

For the Yankees, however, Shea was another universe entirely—a foreign land of subpar playing conditions, roaring airplanes, and empty seats.

Injuries limited Bud Harrelson in 1975, but the Mets' shortstop was still a fan favorite and leader on the ball club. *Photo courtesy of the National Baseball Hall of Fame*

"We were excited about the renovations at Yankee Stadium, but we felt like step-children at Shea," Blomberg wrote. "The home of the Mets was built on a landfill. It was a swamp: cold, windy, and smelly—on the field and in the clubhouse. We could tell early on that life at Shea was going to be no picnic. On our first day of working out there, the field was rough and the noise from the jets flying overhead was a nuisance. But at least we were still in New York City."

When asked about the noise, generated by the airplanes taking off and landing at nearby LaGuardia Airport, Stottlemyre—who was set to pitch in the opener the very next day—was hopeful that it would be a non-issue.

"I hope it doesn't take away any concentration, especially when I'm on the mound," said Stottlemyre, who won sixteen games for the Yankees in 1973. "I'm an airplane watcher you might say, so I might watch them whenever I'm on the bench, but when I'm on the mound I hope my concentration is good enough so that they don't bother me."

For Stottlemyre, that first start would turn out just fine, as the right-hander pitched a complete-game victory, 6-1 over the Cleveland Indians.

While Shea Stadium might have been a haven for pitchers, with its deep alleys in which speedy outfielders could track down long fly balls, the park was particularly unforgiving to left-handed power-hitters, such as Blomberg.

"Shea Stadium was a lousy place to hit, specifically for left-handed hitters, who were used to the short porch at Yankee Stadium," Blomberg wrote. "The ball simply didn't travel there, making it difficult to hit home runs."

It was no easier for the Yankees front office.

"It was a difficult situation all around," said Appel, who had the unenviable task of keeping things calm and cool despite the entire Yankees universe being uprooted. "There were many things that were quite different. Our offices weren't in the ballpark, we were across the street in the park administration building of the World's Fair grounds. It was visiting clubhouse kind of conditions. We were in the Jets locker room, which was remarkably small for a football team. But at least we didn't have to clean out every time we went on the road for the Mets, so I guess it was the best alternative."

While the Yankees' temporary move to Shea was extremely hard on some of their veterans, there were young players coming up who were turning heads of management and fans alike. One of those players was a young, speedy center fielder by the name of Elliott Maddox.

The New Jersey native was a star baseball player at the University of Michigan, where he won the Big Ten batting title as a junior with a .467 batting average. He was originally drafted in the fourth round by the Houston Astros in 1966, but refused to sign. He was then drafted by the Detroit Tigers in 1968 with the twentieth overall pick of the first round, and played for the Tigers in 1970.

He was traded by Detroit to the Washington Senators—who would become the Texas Rangers. However, the Rangers decided to part ways with Maddox and sold him to the Yankees during the 1974 offseason.

"In 1974, Elliott Maddox really came into his own while we were at Shea, and that was partly because Bill Virdon had been a center fielder and recognized the importance of strong defense," Appel said. "So Maddox, out of nowhere, became a very key guy. Virdon had a lot of respect for him and he thought he was a player a lot like Virdon himself was. A guy who could do a lot for the team defensively and what you got as a hitter was a bonus. Elliott hit over .300 for us, so it really was a big bonus."

For the Yankees manager, the biggest thing about Maddox was his ability to get the job done day in and day out.

"He had all the talent that you would want for a major league center fielder and I always respected him a great deal," Virdon remembered. "He always did a good job for me."

Maddox's 1974 performance gave the Yankees a real reason to be extremely optimistic heading into the 1975 season. However, there were a couple of other reasons for that optimism, as well.

The biggest of them all was a prized possession that came to the Yankees as the result of an odd situation following the 1974 World

Series—where the Oakland Athletics defeated the Los Angeles Dodgers in five games. The best of Oakland's fine pitching staff was a man by the name of Jim Hunter, better known to everyone as Catfish. His agent, Jerry Kapstein, accused Athletics owner Charles O'Finley of not sending Hunter's deferred payment to his client on time. Kapstein said that this meant that Hunter's contract with Oakland should be voided, making him a free agent.

The case would go to arbitration—as per an agreement signed by the owners in 1972. The arbitrator, Peter Seitz, agreed with Kapstein, and Hunter was declared a free agent. Most of the teams in Major League Baseball—twenty-three of the twenty-four, in fact—pursued Catfish Hunter.

Hunter was not just another pitcher. He was coming off of a season during which he led the American League with twenty-five victories. It was the fourth straight season that Hunter had won more than twenty games, and he had been rewarded for his excellence with the 1974 Cy Young Award. To say his demand was high was an understatement.

Catfish had been clear to everyone that he was not solely making his decision based on money. He wanted to make sure his family was taken care of in the contract—and he wanted to play on natural grass. More and more stadiums were starting to use artificial turf, and he didn't like that. Then, on New Year's Eve, Hunter made his decision. For the Yankees and their fans, it would be a Happy New Year.

"Hunter took a nineteen-cent Bic pen and signed a five-year contract for about $3.35 million," Appel wrote in his book, *Pinstripe Empire*.

Catfish Hunter was now a Yankee. The six-foot, 190-pound pitcher did not possess an overly powerful right arm, but it was in fact just powerful enough. He was not a flamethrower. Where Hunter separated himself from others was his control, an assortment of pitches, and the heart of a lion.

Virdon was confident that Hunter's new salary would not cause any animosity between him and his new teammates.

"I don't think so," Virdon said. "All of our players will realize having him increases our opportunity to win a pennant and I know that's what they want more than anything."

Years later, former teammate Sparky Lyle was very clear about how little Hunter's salary meant to the other players.

"You never thought about him making that kind of money," Lyle told the *New York Times*. "I don't recall anybody ever thinking about it. You just didn't. You just enjoyed his company. He was just a great person to be around."

One thing was for sure—the Yankees fans were certainly excited with the signing. One week after Hunter used that Bic pen to sign his deal, Yankees season tickets sales rose by 16 percent. It looked like there would be some people in the seats at Shea for Yankees games after all.

The fact that the Yankees made this major acquisition at a time that they were not playing in Yankee Stadium did not make much of a difference, according to the Yankees' Director of PR at the time.

"I don't think that mattered at all; I think they were two distinct things," Appel said. "Hunter's presence was enormous, and the fact that we were playing at Shea didn't really take away from that at all. He was still a towering figure to have on the ball club."

Hunter's arrival was the second of two major reasons for the optimism.

Following the struggles of Bobby Murcer in 1974, Yankees' brass felt it was time for a change. His two lowly home runs at Shea Stadium the previous season, along with his vocal distaste for playing in Queens, made the popular Yankees outfielder easier to trade. However, if the Yankees were going to deal away the popular Murcer, they needed to make sure they got back someone who was considered a star. And they did.

Just days after the 1974 season ended, the San Francisco Giants agreed to send slugger Bobby Bonds to New York in a straight-up, one-for-one trade for Murcer. At the time, Bonds was considered one of the top five offensive players in all of baseball. He had played alongside

Bobby Bonds came to New York in a trade for fan favorite Bobby Murcer before the start of the 1975 season. *Photo courtesy of Larry Ross*

the legendary Willie Mays and was a bona fide slugger. He was two-time all-star and two-time Gold Glover, and he was headed to Shea Stadium for the 1975 season.

• • • •

The Yankees had a rough start to the 1975 season at home, winning just one of their first six games at Shea Stadium. Being on "the road" all the time appeared to be taking its toll early on.

Hunter, New York's prized possession, got off to a very uncharacteristic shaky start himself, losing his first three decisions. He lost the home opener at Shea by a score of 5-3 against the Detroit Tigers. Four days later, Hunter lost another 5-3 decision, this time to the Boston Red Sox, and just like that the Yankees had a record of 1-5. Surely, this was a fluke. Catfish Hunter had won a total of eighty-eight games, while losing just thirty-five over the past four seasons and was the reigning Cy Young Award winner in the American League.

His third start of the season was a rematch against the Detroit Tigers and their star pitcher, Mickey Lolich. However, Hunter lasted only six innings, giving up six earned runs, en route to an 8-3 loss. Three starts into the 1975 season, Catfish Hunter was 0-3.

Things were not much better for the rest of the Yankees. The popular Mel Stottlemyre had gotten injured midway through the 1974 season and was forced to retire. To make matters worse, the team's designated hitter, Ron Blomberg—the first-ever DH—was extremely limited in 1975 with a shoulder injury.

"My shoulder still wasn't right. I tried to play through pain, but my performance on the field reflected my injuries," Blomberg wrote in his biography. "I suffered all kinds of physical problems during the 1975 season and hit only .255, by far the worst of my career, with only four home runs."

Ron Blomberg battled through injuries for much of the Yankees' stay at Shea Stadium and played in only thirty-four games in 1975. *Photo courtesy of the National Baseball Hall of Fame*

Blomberg had been selected by the Yankees with the first overall pick in the 1967 amateur draft. He had been an elite athlete in high school and was recruited by some of the biggest names in the world of college basketball and football. However, he was also a hell of a baseball player, and it was in that direction that Blomberg decided to travel. He also loved the idea of playing in New York City. Blomberg, who is Jewish, reveled in playing in the city where so many Jewish people lived. He was known early on as the "Jewish Mickey Mantle."

"To be able to play in front of eight million Jews, can't beat it," Blomberg once told the publication *The Jewish Standard*. "I lit everyone's candles for every Bar Mitzvah in the city. It was like I was related to everyone. They named a sandwich after me at the Stage Deli."

In 1973, Blomberg became the first major leaguer to appear in a game and not play in the field. The newest "position" in the lineup had been discussed for years by owners to speed up the game and increase team offense, rather than have weak-hitting pitchers come up to bat. Prior to the start of the 1973 campaign, the American League owners voted 8-4 to introduce the designated hitter rule as a three-year trial.

In his first trip to the plate as a designated hitter, Blomberg faced Boston Red Sox star pitcher Luis Tiant. He walked.

By 1975, American League players and fans—and most stadiums—were used to the designated hitter. However, Shea Stadium was a National League ballpark and was not properly outfitted for the new rule—a rule that did not affect its primary tenants, the New York Mets.

"The portion of the scoreboard where you post the lineups did not accommodate for the DH, so we used the letter for 'B' for batter. It couldn't even do a 'D'; it could only do what the positions were," Appel said. "But I always loved that scoreboard. It was easy to find things and easy to read. At Yankee Stadium, we were used to programming a small message board, which was just eight characters by eight lines, so you had to be very efficient with your message. It was nice to have a lot more space."

Marty Appel was a central figure during the Yankees' two-year stay at Shea Stadium. Although he had been a part of the Yankees' front office since 1968 while still in college, he was named the Yankees' public relations director in 1973. At the age of twenty-three, the Brooklyn native was the youngest PR director in league history.

When it was clear that there was no room at Shea Stadium for the Yankees offices, it was Appel's idea to house the offices in Flushing Meadows Park. It was a little more complicated than taking the elevator upstairs, as they had at Yankee Stadium, but at least the front office was able to make the short walk across the park and into the stadium.

Appel would go on to have a storied career as an executive, a public relations czar, and a prolific author. However, by the start of the 1975 baseball season, Appel was just trying to keep things sane for the Yankees. After all, they were only halfway through the longest road trip in history.

• • • •

1975 SCOREBOOK & OFFICIAL MAGAZINE
50¢
TAX INCL.

Four years earlier, it appeared as if the Mets and Yankees would not have any need to share Shea Stadium after all. It looked like a real possibility that the Yankees—and the Yankees alone—might be calling Shea Stadium "home." That's because in 1971, the Mets were strongly considering moving to New Jersey. The whole concept arose when the Yankees were trying to get New York City to renovate Yankee Stadium. Long before the Yankees stopped by Shea Stadium for a two-year stay, one of the options on the table for New York City was to have the Mets and Yankees share Shea Stadium permanently. That option was suggested by Sanford Garelik—the president of the City Council—when the Yankees threatened to leave New York themselves if their stadium was not renovated. Clearly, the Mets were not happy.

"I'm getting a little sick of Mr. Garelik talking about breaking our lease," Mets chairman of the board M. Donald Grant told reporters. "If he is successful breaking our lease, then I would recommend to the board of directors that we either sell out or move the team to New Jersey."

Grant was quick to point out that when the Mets needed someplace to play at the start of 1962, the Yankees refused to share Yankee Stadium, forcing the Mets to play in the crumbling Polo Grounds.

"What did they ever do for us?" Grant said of the Yankees.

What all of this talk did for the Yankees was get them the renovation promises they had been seeking. The Mets would stay in Shea Stadium, ironically sharing the building with the Yankees for the 1974 and 1975 seasons, in spite of Grant.

• • • •

Through the first two months of the 1975 season, the Yankees were playing slightly below .500 baseball, and Catfish had rebounded to win his next six starts. During that time, he gave up only eleven earned runs in 53$\frac{1}{3}$ innings pitched. For the first five games of his winning streak, Hunter pitched complete games, including two shutouts and a ten-inning gem. The pitcher in whom the Yankees had invested so much time—and money—had finally arrived.

Catfish Hunter's twenty-three victories in 1975 gave him five straight years of twenty or more wins. *Photo courtesy of the National Baseball Hall of Fame*

As the calendar turned to June, things appeared to be looking up for the Bombers. Through the first fifty games, Elliott Maddox—the Yankees' up-and-coming center fielder—was on an all-star pace. He was hitting above .300 and playing stellar defense. Thurman Munson was also having a fantastic year at the plate, as the catcher's batting average remained in the high .350s through the first forty-plus games. After getting off to a slow start offensively, third baseman Graig Nettles's bat started to come alive as the weather got warmer and was becoming a force to reckon with on his way to the All-Star Game. Bobby Bonds, the Yankees' other big offseason acquisition, also got off to an extremely slow start with the bat—striking out a ton—but he too started to come alive at the end of May. During a late May/early June Yankees road trip Bonds got extremely hot, batting over .400 with eight home runs during an eleven-game hitting streak.

Toward the middle of the thirteen-game road trip, the Yankees seemed unstoppable, winning eight straight games. They then came home for a ten-game home stand at Shea Stadium that would literally blow up in their faces.

"When you talk about the two years that the Yankees played at Shea, you have to talk about how we almost blew up their ballpark," said Appel, with a hearty laugh.

The first of two memorable events took place on June 10, 1975.

"We had a promotions director named Barry Landers and he was approached for us to do a tribute for the U.S. Army's 200th anniversary. They wanted to have a salute to the U.S. Army Day. General Westmoreland was there, so it was big time. Part of the ceremony was a twenty-one-gun salute from a cannon in the outfield. I wouldn't believe it if I hadn't seen it. There were obviously no cannon balls; it was just the noise and the reverberation knocked down the center field fence."

Watching on television was a Mets fan by the name of Howie Rose. Rose, who was working at New York's Sports Phone at the time, was stunned by what he had seen.

"That's when you really kind of felt that the Mets were being intruded upon, and the way things were going in the Bronx those days there were a lot of jokes at the time—some rather insensitive—about the Yankees bringing the Bronx to Queens," said Rose, who has been a Mets broadcaster for more than twenty years and is considered the foremost authority on Mets' history. "I remember thinking, 'Now what is this riffraff doing coming in and messing up our ballpark?' The Yankees were about as out of place at Shea Stadium as a pork chop at a Bar Mitzvah. It just wasn't a good fit."

Once the smoke cleared and the gaping holes in the outfield fence were revealed, the fans gasped and even cheered. The game that night against the California Angels was delayed, and the night when the Yankees almost blew up Shea Stadium became a footnote.

"There was like a twenty-five-minute delay while they temporarily hoisted the fence and propped it up so we could play the game," Appel remembered. "I just remember seeing Barry out there standing next to the cannon thinking what is he going to do and what a mess we are in here."

Just three nights later, the Yankees found themselves in another mess entirely. This one was not nearly as comedic and not nearly as easy to prop up. Following the Yankees' 2–1 victory over the Chicago White Sox, young phenom outfielder Elliott Maddox was headed to Lenox Hill Hospital on crutches for X-rays on his right knee. He had slipped in the wet outfield at Shea and suffered what appeared to be a severe knee injury.

"Elliott Maddox was a key Shea Stadium Yankee," Appel said. "Ironically, he wrecked his knee largely because of the muddy, soppy conditions that the outfield grass frequently was in."

Elliott Maddox was one of the brightest young stars on the Yankees in 1975 until he injured his leg in the swampy grass at Shea Stadium. *Photo courtesy of the National Baseball Hall of Fame*

The injury that the Yankees feared would keep Maddox out for several weeks was in fact much worse. Maddox damaged ligaments in his right knee and did not return to the Yankees in 1975. However, that was just the beginning of what would become a saga that Maddox and the Yankees—and Mets—would be dealing with for years.

Just after the conclusion of the 1975 season, Maddox sued the City of New York for $1 million, accusing the city of negligent design and inadequate drainage of the playing field at Shea Stadium. It was that negligence, Maddox and his lawyers contended, that caused him to slip on the wet outfield grass. In addition to the $1 million, he also asked for an additional $100,000 on behalf of his wife.

By the time the 1976 season rolled around, with his lawsuit against the City still pending, Maddox started to get a little upset with the Yankees organization. Despite being injured, the speedy centerfielder had been counting on getting a raise. That did not happen, despite Maddox continuing to insist that his injury was not his fault and that his .307 batting average spoke for itself. The Yankees did not agree, however, and there was no raise forthcoming.

"I talked briefly to George Steinbrenner about money the first week of spring training," Maddox told reporters. "I'm trying to be fair about the thing. I don't think they're being fair, but I'm not worried about it anymore."

Maddox was also upset that the Yankees did not allow him to have surgery, but instead had the outfielder wait to see if he could recover to play down the stretch of the 1975 season. Eventually, however, when it was clear Maddox would not be able to return, he underwent the surgery. He then endured a second surgery within the year.

His suit against New York City was later expanded to become a multimillion-dollar lawsuit against the city, the Yankees, and the Mets, since they were lessees of Shea Stadium.

Maddox was not ready for the start of the 1976 season, as he had hoped. Despite having to remain in Florida on the disabled list to rehab his bad right knee, he remained confident.

"I should be ready in a few weeks," Maddox said, as the regular season got under way in early April. "I think I could join the team by the end of this month. I'm starting to progress more rapidly. I'm doing it faster than the doctors expected, faster than I expected. Not as fast as the ball club would like, but I'm going as fast as my body can tolerate. As long as I'm satisfied with my progress, I can't worry about what other people think."

It turned out, Maddox's recovery took much longer than he or anyone else expected. Maddox was limited to playing only eighteen games for the Yankees in 1976, and by 1977, the Yankees were tired of waiting for him to regain his form. Maddox was traded to the Baltimore Orioles, but only played a short time, and prior to the 1978 season, he was, inexplicably—and almost comically—signed as a free agent by the New York Mets. The Mets gave Maddox a five-year contract, worth about $1 million.

His career with the Mets actually started exactly the same way his Yankees career ended. Prior to the 1978 season getting under way, Maddox was placed on the twenty-one-day disabled list with a strained hamstring. If that came as a surprise to the Mets, then shame on them. In the three previous seasons, Maddox had played in only 122 games, while missing 364 contests.

To make matters worse, Maddox still had bad thoughts about playing in the very outfield that had gobbled up his career.

"I'm not saying I won't go out there if there's standing water in the outfield," Maddox told reporters, "but before the opening game of the season, I'm going to walk around the grass and look for my knee. It's out there somewhere. That grass cost me two years of my career."

Unfortunately, although he didn't know it in 1978, it cost him his entire career.

His last hurrah as a player came in 1980. Maddox played in 130 games—115 of which were at third base, not in the outfield—for the Mets that season. It was the most games that Maddox had played in since 1974. It was also the last games that he would play in the majors.

Maddox was never able to recover from that fateful night on the wet outfield grass at Shea Stadium. By 1980, his days as a player were over. Elliott Maddox would always be a "what-might-have-been."

Prior to spring training in 1981, the Mets released Maddox. The Philadelphia Phillies signed him that June, but he never got into uniform.

It wasn't until 1985—ten years after Maddox slipped in Shea's outfield—that the Court of Appeals of the State of New York finally put an end to *Maddox v. City of New York*. In the end, Maddox lost his case.

The official court ruling explained that Maddox knew of the dangers. It read, in part:

"Noting that plaintiff had admitted that the previous night's game had been canceled because of the weather and poor field conditions, that he had during the game in question observed the centerfield to be 'awfully wet' with 'some mud' and standing water above the grass line, had reported that condition to a ground crew member, and had presented no evidence of an order from a superior after making the condition known, it held that there remained no triable issue of fact as to plaintiff's assumption of the risk. Before us, plaintiff argues that he assumed the risks of the game, not of the playing field, which was in an unreasonably dangerous condition, that the risk had in any event been enhanced, that he had no choice but to continue to play, and that the evidence did not establish his subjective awareness that his foot could get stuck in the mud. For the reasons that follow we disagree with that analysis and, therefore, affirm."

• • • •

Following the loss of Maddox in 1975, the Yankees acquired Ed Brinkman from the Texas Rangers and activated Blomberg, in hopes of sparking the offense. Both of those moves failed. Brinkman provided almost no offense at all and Blomberg batted only .255 in thirty-four games. He was already looking to the future. "After spending time at Shea Stadium, I was anxious to play in the new-and-improved Yankee Stadium," he wrote.

However, as July turned into August, the Yankees were not playing to Steinbrenner's expectations. On August 2, following a 5-3 victory over the Cleveland Indians, Bill Virdon was relieved of his managerial duties. Only a handful of people knew about the firing. There was no fanfare, or even an announcement, at the time of Virdon's firing. This would be in stark contrast to the way George Steinbrenner would handle most of his hirings and firings—with the subtlety of a July Fourth fireworks show. Although as fans would soon find out, the announcement would indeed be made in style.

Steinbrenner had given Virdon a chance to make it work in 1975. He had tried to make major improvements to the Yankees' roster, acquiring Catfish Hunter and Bobby Bonds. But the team was floundering at—or slightly above—the .500 mark. When some of the veteran players spoke about the Yankees being "lethargic," that was enough for Steinbrenner, and Virdon's fate was sealed.

As a team, the Yankees were hardly divided about Virdon's firing. There were a few players, such as Pat Dobson, who had been critical of the overall strategy he felt Virdon employed, playing for a big inning instead of chipping away. Most of the players supported Virdon, however.

"I'm hurting for him quite a bit," Maddox said upon hearing the news. "I really liked playing under Bill Virdon. I liked him as a person, I considered him a friend."

In the end, most of the players—including the team's newest stars—realized the business of baseball and that a manager can only do so much.

"A manager might make a difference in five or ten games a year," Catfish Hunter said. "If you're going to win, it's the players who have to do it. I'm sorry to see Bill go. I think he was a heckuva man and a good manager."

Added Bobby Bonds:

"I can't criticize Bill. I respect him. The man was very honest with me and to me. That means a great deal. I don't care what happens with the manager, we as baseball players are still going to have to go out and win. If you have the best players going to the plate with men on third, and they're not bringing them in, that's not the manager's fault."

Virdon's career with the Yankees was over. He was manager for one full season, and just over five months of a second season. He had never stepped foot into Yankee Stadium wearing the pinstripes. He has no regrets.

"I look back only as having fond memories," Virdon said. "I always enjoyed being there and I always knew that [my players] were going to be dependable. They were all excellent and I enjoyed working with all of them. They never let me down."

• • • •

When George Steinbrenner first purchased the New York Yankees from CBS in 1973, he vowed not to be a hands-on owner. He had other, much more qualified baseball people to take charge of the day-to-day baseball activities—people such as Michael Burke, who had been the president of the Yankees since 1966. Burke, a former Navy officer, CIA agent, and general manager of Ringling Bros. and Barnum & Bailey Circus, had been an executive at CBS since 1956.

After being named vice president in charge of developing new areas of business expansion at the television network, one of the first things Burke did at CBS was recommend that the network underwrite a new Broadway show. That show turned out to be *My Fair Lady*.

In the early 1960s, Burke suggested to CBS that they consider purchasing the New York Yankees, which they did in 1966. He had not only been the president of the Yankees from a baseball point of view since then, but he was the driving force in convincing New York City and the mayor to approve the multimillion-dollar renovation plans for Yankee Stadium. That renovation was scheduled to get under way following the 1973 season and it was estimated that the rebuilding of the stadium would cost around $24 million. In the end, that was a dreadful underestimation, but the deal kept the Yankees in New York. Burke and ownership had used the renovation as leverage, hinting at the possibility that perhaps New Jersey would be willing to provide the team a better playing facility. It was more than an idle threat, as the New York football Giants proved.

Now, as CBS was getting set to sell the Yankees, the network wanted to make sure Michael Burke was going to be able to remain in his capacity. At a meeting to finalize the sale, Steinbrenner made a promise to CBS chief executive William S. Paley that he would allow Burke to absolutely do what he did best—run the New York Yankees.

"I can assure you we wouldn't want it any other way," Steinbrenner said. "I've got a ship company to run. I won't have much time for baseball, so Mike will have to carry the load."

Satisfied, Paley agreed to sell the Yankees to Steinbrenner for what ended up being around $8.8 million. Although the cost has very often been reported at $10 million, the deal had included two parking garages, which CBS had purchased from New York City. After the deal with Steinbrenner was official, New York City bought the parking garages back from the Yankees.

The Steinbrenner regime had begun. At the January 3 press conference to introduce the Cleveland ship-magnate as the new owner of the New York Yankees, Steinbrenner told the world of his intentions.

"We plan absentee ownership as far as running the Yankees. We're not going to pretend we're something we aren't. I'll stick to building ships."

Steinbrenner's words—at the time—may have been sincere, or not. Either way, it really didn't matter, as he was the owner. He wasn't yet "The Boss"—that would take a few more years—but he was the owner, and it became clear very fast that not everything Steinbrenner said ended up being reality.

After a tumultuous four months, fighting over everything from player contracts to fresh-cut flowers in Burke's office, Steinbrenner had had enough of his president by July. The man who was going to handle day-to-day operations for the Yankees and oversee the renovation of Yankee Stadium—was out.

Burke went on to become the president of Madison Square Garden and signed a five-year contract that gave him the title of president of both the New York Knickerbockers and the New York Rangers.

In the Bronx—well, in Queens—the "absentee owner" was now in charge.

• • • •

Old-Timers Day for the Yankees took place one day after firing Virdon. It was certainly an odd sight to see players such as Joe DiMaggio, Whitey Ford, Mickey Mantle, and Yogi Berra honored in pinstripes crossing the field at Shea Stadium. That was the reality in 1975, however. Besides, there was something that was about to happen that would shock the Yankee fans, no matter what stadium they were calling home.

Normally, public address announcer Bob Sheppard—the stadium voice of the Yankees since 1951—would introduce DiMaggio last. However, not on this day. Following DiMaggio, there was one more introduction:

"Number One, the new manager of the New York Yankees . . . Billy Martin," Sheppard announced.

Martin walked out onto the field wearing a cowboy jacket, pants, and boots. The crowd went crazy and gave him a standing ovation. Eighteen years earlier, the Yankees had crushed Martin by trading the second baseman away. Now, in 1975, he was back.

Martin had been a solid player for the Yankees throughout the 1950s and a star player in World Series play. He was like a brother to Mickey Mantle and was a fan favorite. Earlier in 1975, Martin was fired as the manager of the Texas Rangers. He had previously managed the Detroit Tigers and Minnesota Twins. When the Rangers dismissed him, Steinbrenner pounced on the fiery manager. Being hired to manage the Yankees was the start of a raucous relationship between Martin and Steinbrenner, professionally and personally. However, in 1975, Martin's number-one concern was getting the Yankees back on the winning track.

He would spend the next two months observing everything about the team, what made them good, what was holding them back, so that when 1976 rolled around, he would have the team he wanted to put on the field. He didn't care about a player's reputation; he cared about a player's drive and guts.

When Bobby Bonds went to Martin and pulled himself out of a lineup late in 1975 because one of his legs was bothering him, Bonds sealed his fate for being traded before the following season. Sure enough, during the offseason Bonds was moved to the California Angels for Ed Figueroa and Mickey Rivers. Martin did not want to hear what a player *couldn't* do, but rather what he was going to do to *help* his team.

The Yankees ended up playing only slightly better for Billy Martin for the remainder of the season as they had for Bill Virdon, finishing up four games above .500 for the new skipper.

One thing was for sure, however; Catfish Hunter had certainly shown everyone the type of pitcher he really was. Despite starting the season losing his first three games, Hunter posted a 23-14 record, his fifth-straight season winning twenty or more games. His twenty-three victories led the American League, as did his *thirty* complete games, 328 innings pitched, and 1,294 batters faced. Hunter also posted an impressive 2.58 earned run average. Remarkably, those numbers were not enough to earn Catfish his second-straight Cy Young Award in the American League. That honor went to Baltimore star hurler Jim Palmer. The two had very comparable statistics, but in the end, it was Palmer who walked away with the award.

"Catfish Hunter was the cornerstone of the Yankees' success over the last quarter century," Yankees owner George Steinbrenner would say years later. "We were not winning before Catfish arrived . . . He exemplified class and dignity and he taught us how to win."

As a team, the Yankees won nine of their final twelve games at Shea Stadium and finished the season with a record of 83-77, only good enough for third place in the American League East. However, the Yankees left Shea Stadium with a bang—not that any fences were in danger this time. Still, the team's final home game in 1975 was one of the most memorable and exciting games of the entire season.

The Yankees entered the bottom of the ninth trailing Mike Flanagan and the Baltimore Orioles 2-0. It was the second game of a doubleheader, and Baltimore had taken the opener by a score of 3-0. It seemed clear that the Yankees had little left to play for—little left in their tanks. It seemed certain that 1975 would end with a doubleheader sweep and most likely, back-to-back shutout losses.

Then, Billy Martin saw a glimpse of the future.

Roy White led off the bottom of the ninth with a single to center field on an 0-2 pitch. The next batter was catcher Thurman Munson, who also singled, sending White to third base. Rick Dempsey followed Munson by drawing a walk to load the bases. Baltimore manager Earl Weaver had seen enough of Flanagan, who had pitched eight-plus innings of brilliant baseball. However, Flanagan had nothing left and Weaver went to his bullpen for Dyar Miller. Martin countered by pinch-hitting Chris Chambliss for Otto Velez.

The first chess move of the inning went to Weaver, as Miller struck out Chambliss. The next scheduled hitter was Rick Bladt, but Martin went to his bench again, and sent up Terry Whitfield as a pinch-hitter. This time, Martin's move came up aces as Whitfield stroked a single to right field, scoring White and Munson. The game was now tied at two.

Martin had one last move. He sent up a third-straight pinch-hitter in Rich Coggins, who was sent up to bat for Ed Brinkman with one out and the winning run on third base. However, Coggins never had to do a thing. Dyar Miller stunned Rick Dempsey with a pickoff throw to third base, but the throw was wild and headed past everyone, Dempsey raced home with the winning run, and the Yankees had a 3-2 victory.

As Dempsey stepped on Shea Stadium's home plate, it all came to a thrilling end—two years of road games, two years of soggy Shea, and two years of the smelly Jets locker room.

There were clearly going to be brighter days ahead for the Yankees. They just wouldn't be in Queens.

CHAPTER 3

Big Shea

"THE BUSIEST CORNER OF NEW York yesterday may have been the dozen-acre plot in Queens known as Shea Stadium," Joseph Durso wrote in the *New York Times* on April 10, 1975. "No baseball game was played there, but three of the 24 teams in the major leagues converged on the year for 90-minute workouts with assembly-line precision."

And so it began in 1975 for Shea Stadium. On this day, the New York Mets took the field for a workout at 11 a.m. for their afternoon game against the Philadelphia Phillies. Their new roommates, meanwhile, the New York Yankees, took the field at 1 p.m. to warm up for their home game the following day against the Detroit Tigers. Finally, at 2:30 p.m. the Phillies were able to take a turn in the field.

"Tonight," Durso quoted Mets ace pitcher Tom Seaver as saying, "the Jets will work out here and that'll make an even four teams." Of course, Seaver was just joking around, but the sentiment was very real. Shea Stadium may well have been re-named Grand Central Terminal for the 1975 campaign.

• • • •

Shea Stadium was a very special place to New Yorkers from the day it opened in 1964—especially fans of the Mets and Jets. It was their shiny new home, with all of the amenities that teams, players, and fans could hope for.

There was the impressive new scoreboard, which showed color slides of the players' faces when they came to bat. It displayed out of town scores for both the National and American leagues. And it was able to display full messages to the fans in attendance. It was a techno-logical marvel that seemed like it belonged beyond the outfield walls in a display at the New York World's Fair.

There were the fifty-four shiny new restrooms—twenty-seven for men and twenty-seven for women—twenty-one escalators, and four public restaurants. The final bill for Shea was $24.5 million, with the Mets chipping in an additional $6.5 million for their own office space, clubhouses, scoreboard, restaurants, and pressroom.

"What it lacked," author Curt Smith wrote, "was a spitspot of charm."

All of the seats in the new stadium were wooden, with each level having a different color. The vast majority of seating was positioned between the foul poles, and most of the seats were angled to point directly to center field. This was not exactly optimum for baseball. Field box seats were yellow, loge seats were brown, mezzanine seats were blue, and upper deck seats were green. To make things easier for fans attending a game in the new ballpark, game tickets and signs in each seating area were color-coded according to the seat you had.

"My family moved from the Bronx to Bayside, Queens, in 1962, which is not that far from where Shea Stadium was being erected," said Howie Rose, the Mets broadcaster who knows more about Mets history than anyone else—mostly because he lived it himself. "On more than one occasion, my dad, my uncle, my cousin, and myself actually went there and stood on the opposite side of Roosevelt Avenue from where the ballpark was being built and really just watched it take shape. I had a pretty good working knowledge of what that place looked like step-by-step, incrementally along the way to its completion. So there was a lot of anticipation."

"By the time I was twelve, I remember Opening Day, 1966, was the first game I went to without adult supervision, just with some friends. Once those shackles came off, Shea Stadium was every bit the home to me that the apartment we lived in was. I felt very comfortable and very much at home there and spent enough time at that ballpark where they probably could have sent my mail there and I probably would have gotten it. It was very much home and very much became a part of my DNA really."

In fact, the construction of Shea Stadium drew positive and negative feedback from politicians, architects, union reps, and—of course—the press. Why were they building this stadium, some pondered? Did New York City need this stadium and this baseball team? One of the writers asking this loudly was newspaper writer Jimmy Breslin, who wondered why New York City needed to go to all the trouble to build "a brand-new stadium for Marvin Throneberry."

Critics aside, by the time Shea Stadium was officially dedicated on April 16, 1964, more than 1,000 people turned out to hear the Department of Sanitation Band play "Take Me Out to the Ball Game" and watch Robert Moses, Mayor Robert Wagner, Casey Stengel, and—of course—Bill Shea himself declare the stadium open for business.

Even the opposing teams were impressed with the new building.

"Shea Stadium is a showplace," said former Pittsburgh Pirates manager Danny Murtaugh. "This will become one of the must-see places for all tourists to New York, like the Empire State Building, Radio City, or the Statue of Liberty."

Not everything was rosy, of course. The day after the Mets lost their first Shea Stadium home opener, in 1964 to the Pirates, the headline in the *New York Times* shouted: "50,312 attend opener at Shea Stadium; Lack of parking causes backups." Future Hall of Famer Willie Stargell registered the first hit at Shea and later, the first home run at Shea.

Just six days earlier, demolition had begun on the outdated former home of the Mets, Jets, Giants, and Yankees, located north of 155th Street in Manhattan on a piece of land known as Coogan's Bluff.

There were several incarnations of the Polo Grounds, but the final one—which was now being demolished—served its teams well from 1911 through 1963. It was the home of the Yankees from 1913 through 1922, when the team moved—thanks to a slugger named Babe Ruth—into its own house across the river in the Bronx.

The baseball Giants played their final home game there on September 22, 1957 and headed west to California with the Brooklyn Dodgers. The stadium was never really kept up following the Giants' departure, and by the time the Mets arrived in 1962, it was literally falling apart. It was a fitting end to see the Polo Grounds meet the wrecking ball a week before Shea Stadium was opened. There was a genuine feeling—some nostalgia aside—of out with the old and in with the new.

· · · ·

The idea of a new ballpark in the borough of Queens goes back as far as 1940. However, when Moses, Mayor Wagner, New York attorney William A. Shea, and others finally got their stadium approved, it was July of 1958. There was no team to place in the new stadium, but New York City hierarchy was confident that if it had a place to put a team, it would be able to get a team—most likely through expansion.

The president of the National League at the time, Warren C. Giles, seemed to be a willing partner.

"Growing out of past discussions of the matters," Giles said, "and the statement by Mr. Shea, chairman of Mayor Wagner's baseball committee, with Mayor Wagner present and concurring, that the City of New York is able and willing to provide modern baseball facilities at the Flushing Meadows location, the following resolution was adopted . . . "

That resolution appointed several people to a committee—headed by Shea—that would weigh the benefits of expanding the National League from eight teams to ten. The mayor was more than overjoyed.

"It will be for the best interests of all [of] baseball to have the National League back in New York," Mayor Wagner stated, reminding

New Yorkers of something they needed no reminder of—the fact that the Dodgers and Giants had bolted to the sunny skies of California.

A major part of the mayor's willingness to build the new stadium was that it was going to be financed legally, without violating the city's self-imposed prohibition against borrowing money "for the building of a stadium, or docks, or anything similar." According to Mayor Wagner, the law permitted the city to borrow the $12 million necessary to build the stadium because there is a provision for self-liquidation of the debt, which would be through a yearly rental and through amortization over a time span of twenty years.

By today's standards, it was pocket change, but in 1958, it was a rental and amortization that appeared to be an extremely heavy load for any baseball team to assume. The prevailing belief, however, was that since an expansion team would not cost the owners anything to purchase, those owners would be able to handle the stadium costs ahead of them. Experts felt that the best number to place on the tenant baseball team would be $900,000 annually.

That number might be acceptable for a new, expansion team, but would definitely be something of a burden to an existing team if it moved from another city to take up residence in Queens. However, the general manager of the St. Louis Cardinals, Bing Devine, spoke openly about those chances. "There is no indication that anybody wants to go to New York at the moment," he said snidely. But was Devine correct?

Just a month or so later, Cincinnati Reds owner Powel Crosley hinted that perhaps his Reds would consider making the move East and set up shop in New York. Unfortunately for Shea, Crosley was only playing chicken with the city of Cincinnati. He had been upset that there was not enough parking at Crosley Field and decided to take advantage of the situation in New York City. Soon after Crosley hinted that his team may move, the city of Cincinnati agreed to tear down some of the buildings near the stadium, which would allow Crosley to now have an additional 2,400 parking spots. There was no additional talk of the Reds going anywhere.

Still, the stadium plan in New York City moved forward without a team. Despite not having a team, the new stadium would have something that no one could have imagined—a retractable roof. In April of 1960, Shea, as the chairman of the Mayor's Special Committee on Baseball, announced that the new stadium in Flushing Meadows Park would indeed have a dome covering it in time for Opening Day in 1962. The retractable dome was going to be made of aluminum or lightweight steel and would add about $3.5 million to the stadium costs. Those additional costs would not be the burden of the city nor of the team, however. While the team would be responsible for paying the rent for the stadium, the dome costs would be paid for by raising private capital from investors. Until that capital was raised, Shea asked the aluminum and steel companies to allow the city to defer payment on the construction of the dome. According to Shea's initial statement, the chances of the new stadium having a dome were "increasingly strong."

"We would draw all kinds of events there if we get the dome," Shea said. "That would help us pay the rent on the stadium."

Although, he admitted soon thereafter, that the chances were more like 50-50.

Confidence was never an issue for Bill Shea, who for five decades was a close confidant of governors, mayors, and corporate leaders alike. His connections and his guile allowed him to build one of New York's largest and most influential law firms, Shea & Gould. In addition, these qualities made him a good fit to not only make sure a stadium was built, but also to find a team to call that stadium home.

"He is the city's most experienced power broker, its premier matchmaker," Nicholas Pileggi wrote about Shea in a 1974 profile in *New York* magazine, "a man who spent 40 years turning the orgies of politicians, bankers, realtors, union chiefs, underwriters, corporate heads, utility combines, cement barons, merchant princes and sports impresarios into profitable marriages."

Pileggi described Shea as "the unofficial chairman of the state's unofficial permanent government," and as someone who throughout his career had "labored quietly in a political twilight somewhere between the private interest and the public good."

Shea—with Mayor Wagner's support and blessing—had a solution for not having a team to play at the new stadium. With the National League dragging its feet, the duo announced that New York City would join a third major league, which Shea originally proposed and formed in 1959, known as the Continental League. Other Continental League teams would be in Denver, Houston, Minneapolis, and Toronto. Legendary baseball executive Branch Rickey would be the league's president and play was scheduled to begin in 1961.

It was a power play. Shea was not afraid to play his hand and wait for others to fold. He was a great competitor himself, having been a scholarship athlete at New York University and then Georgetown University—starring in lacrosse and football.

"Shea was neither a litigator nor a legal scholar. Rather, he was the sort of lawyer whom powerful men trusted with their secrets and whom they could rely upon as a go-between. He was adept at putting people at ease, and despite his outgoing nature, never offending. He was the kind of man people liked. He earned a reputation as a man who could get things done."

Shea lived up to that reputation. By July of 1960, representatives from the National and American leagues requested to meet with Rickey to discuss possible baseball expansion plans. The possibility of the Continental League being a threat to Major League Baseball was not being brushed off by the game's leaders; it was in fact scaring them. Owners of what would be the Continental League teams had no interest in being absorbed by the majors.

"The Continental League was founded upon the need of many large cities in our country for major league baseball," Rickey told reporters. "The Continental League as now constituted is prepared to bring about that expansion."

Rickey—like Shea—was not one to back down from confrontations. He had done just about everything a man could have done in Major League Baseball. The Ohio native was a weak-hitting catcher in the majors from 1905–1914. He was the manager and general manager for the St. Louis Browns—the team he was playing for—from 1913–1915. He then went on to become the manager and general manager of the crosstown St. Louis Cardinals from 1919–1925. Rickey left the dugout following the 1925 season, but continued on as the Cardinals' general manager until the end of the 1942 season.

The following season, Rickey (already known as a baseball innovator) took the job as the general manager of the Brooklyn Dodgers. He held that role from 1943–1950, literally changing the face of the game. He then went on to be the general manager of the Pittsburgh Pirates from 1950–1955. To say the least, Branch Rickey's résumé was an impressive one. In addition to his player relations, he is given credit for developing the modern-day farm system, was the first person to establish a full-time spring training facility, and—way ahead of his time—encouraged teams to use things such as batting cages, pitching machines, and helmets.

But the old man was seventy-eight now, taking up a new baseball cause—for a bunch of baseball-starved cities. He and Shea were holding firm, fully prepared to move forward the Continental League. The hard line worked. Just days after Rickey met with the league presidents, it became clear that both the National and American leagues were ready to expand from eight teams each to ten teams each.

The decision was not quite final, but cities involved started to get excited.

Former St. Louis Cardinals great Marty Marion—the Most Valuable Player of the 1944 World Series—was part owner of the Houston Buffs of the American Association. He was overjoyed that his city might be joining the elite of the major leagues.

"This is a great day for Houston," said Marion, who in his day was as good a shortstop as there was. "We are on the verge of big league baseball."

By August of 1960, it was official. Before a single pitch was ever thrown in the Continental League, the American and National leagues finally announced that they would expand. Ironically, it was Walter

O'Malley, the owner of the Los Angeles Dodgers, who took the podium at the front of the room of gentlemen that included Rickey and Shea, as well as the owners of the other Continental League teams.

"There is only one move open, we must compromise," O'Malley stated. "We will take four of your cities and later add the rest."

The American League would add the Los Angeles Angels and a new Washington Senators team in 1961. The original Washington Senators franchise moved to Minnesota and became the Twins that same year. New York City and Houston would be added to the National League in time for the 1962 season.

Soon after the announcement, a reporter asked Rickey if the developments meant that the Continental League was done. "Obviously," he answered.

"My principal mission from the start has been to assure New York of having every-day baseball again," Shea said. "Today's action gives us that assurance and makes it more urgent than ever for the city to proceed with the construction of the new stadium in Flushing Meadows."

The big question was—would New York's new stadium be ready for New York's new baseball team come Opening Day 1962? Absolutely yes, Mayor Wagner assured everyone in January of 1961: "Speaking for all of the board members, we are very pleased with the progress that is being made." However, ground would not be broken on the new stadium for another nine months.

According to New York City Controller Lawrence E. Gerosa, "if construction on the stadium started in the fall of 1960, they would still have to have worked overtime to finish it in time for the 1962 season."

Gerosa—not the mayor—ended up being correct. The new ballpark that would be the home of the New York Metropolitan Baseball Club, to be known as the Mets, would not be close to completion by Opening Day 1962.

The Mets were forced to play their inaugural season at the rickety, old Polo Grounds—abandoned by the baseball Giants following the 1957 season. After decaying for two years with no tenants, the Polo Grounds was inhabited by the American Football League's New York

Titans beginning in 1960. Now, the Mets would join the Titans for the 1962 season.

They also were forced to start their second season there, although officials were extremely confident that by the summer of 1963, the sophomore team could move into their new dorm.

"August is a real good date," said William J. Tooley, the city's stadium director.

"We have enough hope to print tickets for this season," said Jim Thompson, the Mets' business manager.

"It will open in 1963," said Newbold Morris, the Commissioner of Parks.

Unfortunately, that would not happen in 1963. The Mets were forced to play another full season in the decrepit old stadium, as were the Titans—who were now known as the New York Jets. However, according to one of the architects, it would be well worth the wait.

"It will be one of the most modern, comfortable, and architecturally revolutionary stadiums in the country," said Robert H Schoenfeld, who was an engineer for Praeger-Kavanagh-Waterbury.

Fans of the Mets and Jets would have to wait until the World's Fair arrived in 1964 to enjoy the revolutionary stadium.

"The New York World's Fair is preparing programs for the stadium during 1964-65," according to the official New York City Department of Parks program. "There will be many events at the Stadium supplementing the educational exhibits and excitement of the Fair. . . . The Department of Parks, working with Fair Management, is proud to bring to the people of New York this great new [stadium]."

Two years late, or—for World's Fair President Robert Moses—perhaps right on time.

• • • •

"I'm English and I knew nothing about baseball, so [to me] Shea Stadium was never this baseball legend at all," said rock superstar Sting, who in the 1970s and 1980s was the lead singer for the hugely popular group, the Police. "[To me], it was where the Beatles played."

When the Beatles took the stage on that hot summer night in 1965, having a rock band perform in a stadium was a completely new experience. However, the arrival of the Beatles in America and the arrival of Shea Stadium in New York made the pairing a no-brainer for concert promoters.

"I called the man that I was negotiating with and said 'forget Madison Square Garden, I think I'm going to take them to Shea Stadium'," said concert promoter Sid Bernstein.

More than 55,000 delirious fans, who paid about $5 each to gain entry, packed into the ballpark to watch the groundbreaking concert, and immediately drowned out the band's vocals with their own deafening screams. Fainting girls and audience members attempting to reach the stage kept the numerous security guards occupied. It was the most chaotic, raucous concert that New Yorkers had ever experienced. The Beatles were preceded on stage by a number of opening acts, including Brenda Holloway, Cannibal and the Headhunters, King Curtis, Sounds Incorporated, and the Young Rascals.

The 55,600 fans set a world record for attendance and gross revenue, netting the band $160,000. It was the opening show of the group's second tour of the United States. Taking the stage at 9:16 p.m., they slammed through twelve songs in just over a half an hour. Their set list at Shea was the same as it would be for the Beatles' entire tour of the United States: "Twist and Shout," "She's a Woman," "I Feel Fine," "Dizzy Miss Lizzy," "Ticket to Ride," "Everybody's Trying to Be My Baby," "Can't Buy Me Love," "Baby's in Black," "Act Naturally," "A Hard Day's Night," "Help!", and "I'm Down." The event was filmed for a television special, first seen on March 1, 1966.

"I was a little too young, regrettably, to attend the Beatles concerts," Mets broadcaster and historian Howie Rose said. "I wish to this day that I could have gone. If there is one event that I wish that I could have gone to at Shea—other than a baseball game—it would have been a Beatles concert."

Following the historic 1965 concert was a much lesser known second Shea Stadium Beatles concert one year later, on August 23, 1966.

This time, the Beatles did not sell out Shea, but they did make more money, reportedly receiving $189,000. The Beatles played eleven songs: "Rock and Roll Music," "She's a Woman," "If I Needed Someone," "Day Tripper," "Baby's in Black," "I Feel Fine," "Yesterday," "I Wanna Be Your Man," "Nowhere Man," "Paperback Writer," and "Long Tall Sally."

"Curiously enough the second Shea Stadium concert had about 11,000 seats unsold," Beatles producer George Martin was quoted as saying in *The Beatles Anthology*. "So it was a pretty unsettling time. And it was against this background that they said, 'Right, we definitely won't do any more. We are going to have a break and then we are going into the studio to make a record.'"

Almost exactly seventeen years later—on August 18, 1983—the Police had a concert of their own added to the Shea Stadium schedule. Tickets for the show sold out in less than five hours. The 70,000 fans that came to rock with the Police comprised the greatest number of people to ever witness an event at Shea Stadium. The Police had two opening acts—the well-known Joan Jett and the Blackhearts—and a small band from Athens, Georgia simply known as R.E.M.

"We'd like to thank the Beatles for lending us their stadium," Sting said toward the end of the concert.

The *New York Times* concert review from that night lauded the band:

> It is a good sign that the Police can draw so many people and satisfy them, because the band's music works radical changes on what rock-arena audiences came to expect in the 1970's. The band's songs are light, not ponderous; introspective rather than aggressive; syncopated, not stomping, and more clever than simple-minded. Sting's lyrics even drop names like Nabokov and Scylla and Charybdis.
>
> What makes the Police stand out among performing bands is that it never bothers to imitate its records. The trio couldn't if it tried, since band members overdub extra instruments in the recording studio. So it goes to the other extreme, revamping every song in a gleeful whirl of improvisation. The Police is one of the few rock bands—along with

the Rolling Stones, the Talking Heads and the Grateful Dead—that is willing to shake up its arrangements nightly.

Throngs of people and positive reviews notwithstanding, it was on stage that very night, not far from the pitching mound from which Tom Seaver had led the Mets to a World Championship, that Sting decided he needed a change. It was during that concert that the rock icon decided it was time for the mega-hit band the Police to break up.

"That was the point where I realized that it can't get better than this, you can't climb a higher mountain than this, this was Everest," said Sting, describing the feeling he had playing at Shea Stadium. "I made the decision on stage [at Shea] that this is where this thing stops."

Shea Stadium had always been a destination that attracted some of the biggest and brightest stars in the music industry. Clearly, there was a lot of interest in playing at the "top of Everest," or playing where the Beatles had played.

In August of 1970, Shea Stadium was the site for the Summer Festival for Peace, which was a day-long fundraiser featuring performers such as Janis Joplin, Paul Simon, Creedence Clearwater Revival, and Miles Davis. Throughout the 1970s and early 1980s, bands such as Grand Funk Railroad, Humble Pie, Jethro Tull, The Who, The Clash, and Simon & Garfunkel graced the Shea infield.

The Rolling Stones would play six sold-out nights at Shea in 1989 as part of their Steel Wheels Tour, supported by the new band, Living Colour. A few years later, Elton John and Eric Clapton played there together in 1992 and Bruce Springsteen and E Street Band performed at Big Shea in 2003.

The final concert at Shea Stadium was a 2008, two-night mega event by Long Island native Billy Joel, who sold out both of his July shows in under an hour. Joel invited many of music's biggest names to join him on stage—including Tony Bennett, Steven Tyler, Jon Mayer, Garth Brooks, and Robert Plant—so that he could close Shea in style. His most special guest was Sir Paul McCartney, who thirty-four years earlier had really gotten the whole music thing started at Shea Stadium with his fellow Beatles band members. McCartney performed songs with Joel, and it was actually McCartney who closed down Shea's music legacy by performing "Let It Be."

．．．．

The gentleman who drove McCartney from his dressing room to the stage in 2008 was the same gentleman who in 1965 drove the Beatles from the stage in a white station wagon with the Mets logo emblazed on the sides, to an awaiting car beyond the center field fence. However, being a chauffeur was not Pete Flynn's main responsibility. The native of Ballinamore, County Leitrim, Ireland, actually had a few more things on his to-do list.

When baseball returned to the Polo Grounds in 1962, Flynn found his life's work. He helped build the advance ticket booth at the Polo Grounds. "Then I went out on the field and stayed there," he said. He was hired by Johnny McCarthy to be a lead groundskeeper for the Mets. He also served the same function that fall for the New York Titans of the American Football League. When the teams moved to Shea Stadium in 1964, Flynn moved as well and eventually was named as the head groundskeeper in 1974.

One year later, Flynn and his staff had the challenge of their lives.

"Forget about it," Flynn said of the 1975 season. "Once the football season started, there was not much we could do. You didn't have any time because it was every week."

Since Shea Stadium did not re-sod the infield for football, the Jets and Giants—and their opponents—played with half of their field on the dirt infield.

"Back then they didn't sod the infields," Flynn said. "So there was dirt on the field, and in the end zone area."

One of the biggest challenges in keeping Shea looking and playing good throughout the 1975 season had everything to do with water. When it rained, the drainage was poor and Shea would often become a swampy mess in the outfield. And when the field needed water, it was a task and a half to make sure the grass got what it needed. There was no irrigation system at Shea Stadium and no underground sprinklers. This made things extremely laborious for Flynn and his men.

"We had hoses and we had six different areas that we could hook the hoses up to," Flynn said. "Back then we didn't have a sprinkler system. We didn't have a sprinkler system at Shea until the late 1980s."

Still, Flynn did more than survive the 1975 season—he established himself as, quite simply, one of the best in the business. Flynn became synonymous with the Mets and Shea Stadium. And the players all loved him.

"He was one those people that just lit up your life," Hall of Fame Mets pitcher Tom Seaver said in a televised interview. "I love the guy, absolutely love him."

Flynn was more than just a groundskeeper to the Mets, especially the ones that had known him since the beginning—he was family. His job with the Mets actually helped launch his own family, as well. His first year on the job, Flynn met and went on to marry the sister of another groundskeeper. They had two daughters and were together for forty years—living, of course, in Queens.

"Pete was a great guy, and as a head groundskeeper, he was as good as you could get," said Ed Kranepool, who was an original member of the New York Mets, playing until 1979. "He would cater to the players. If I had a problem at first base, I would talk to Pete and he would make any adjustments on the fly. He always took great care of us, and that's why we took care of him in return. They kept the field in good condition. The grounds crew really did a great job maintaining it. There were definitely some spots in the outfield that suffered from overuse, but those guys worked overtime and did a fantastic job."

It seemed that just about all of the Mets had a great relationship with Flynn and his crew.

"Pete and I used to get into water fights all the time with pails of water underneath the stadium," said Jerry Koosman, who was the Mets' ace left-hander. "Sometimes it got out onto the field and sometimes I would grab the hose while they were working on the field and just surprise them and spray them. We had a lot of fun. I remember on the really hot days, the grounds crew would go get a watermelon and they'd have watermelon after they got the field ready and the game had started. Sometimes I would stop on my way to the game and pick up a watermelon for them if I remembered. Sometimes I would sit down and enjoy it with them for a couple of minutes."

Flynn's greatest memories of Shea revolved around two of the greatest and most memorable seasons the stadium's two main tenants ever had.

"The 1968 season with the Jets was just great," Flynn said. "Obviously the 1969 Mets was the best memory I have."

• • • •

Shea Stadium was built to be a multi-purpose baseball and football facility; however in reality was well-equipped to handle just about any athletic event.

From its earliest days, Shea Stadium proved that it was not only a good football venue, but a more than adequate *futbol* stadium as well. The soccer field at Shea was positioned from center field to home plate. Brazil played England in a soccer match on June 17, 1965, as part of the International Soccer League. Eleven years later, Argentina met Italy on June 22, 1976.

On August 17, 1976, soccer legend Pelé and his New York Cosmos played the Washington Diplomats in a North American Soccer League opening round playoff game. Pelé scored the first goal of the game to help lift the Cosmos to a 2-0 victory as 22,698 rejoiced.

It would be another twenty years before Shea Stadium would host another soccer game, as Columbia hosted Honduras in 1996, El Salvador in 1997, and Slovakia in 2003.

For a very brief window in the mid-1960s, prizefighting took center stage—or center infield—at Shea Stadium. With the boxing ring located in the middle of the infield, Jose "Chegui" Torres defeated Wayne Thornton in fifteen rounds to defend his Light Heavyweight Championship in 1966. One year later, Carlos Ortiz defended his own Light Heavyweight title against Ismael Laguna in a fifteen-round victory. The final title fight to take place at Shea occurred on September 29, 1967, when Emile Griffith won a fifteen-round middleweight championship decision over Italy's legendary boxer Nino Benvenuti.

Boxing was replaced at Shea Stadium by a much different type of ring in the 1970s, as Shea played host to three professional wrestling cards. Popular wrestling icons such as Bruno Sammartino, André the Giant, and Hulk Hogan all entertained huge crowds at Shea Stadium.

Baseball, football, soccer, boxing, or wrestling. You name the sport, and it was no problem for Shea.

By far the oddest athletic event to grace the field at big Shea occurred on a sultry week in June of 1967. In the late 1960s, the Ice Capades skating shows had perfected and patented the use of a portable ice rink. Known as "tanks," these rinks could be installed virtually anywhere. That was a good fit for Shea Stadium, which was willing to play host to virtually any event. Ice Capades put down ice at Shea Stadium and performed for 28,233 people, the largest attendance of any ice show in history.

While sports are often considered religion to many, Shea Stadium served as the home base for many actual religious events during the 1970s.

In 1971, the Reverend Billy Graham held his Crusade at Shea Stadium. Like many baseball hitters, Reverend Graham was not happy with the loud roar of the jet engines that were buzzing in and out of nearby LaGuardia Airport. However, unlike the sluggers, Reverend Graham did more than simply step out of the batter's box.

On the opening night of training for the Crusade and after a particularly loud plane passed over the field, Reverend Graham glanced up and said, "We'll have to do something about this noise. This just won't do." Sure enough, as explained in a Graham biography, the next day the winds had miraculously shifted, causing LaGuardia to use different runways, avoiding the flight paths above Shea Stadium.

In July of 1978, the International Convention of Jehovah's Witnesses converged on Queens. Shea Stadium was completely sold out for five nights and a pool for baptizing the faithful was constructed on top of home plate and the batter's boxes. More than 400 people were baptized.

One year later, in the second-ever papal visit to the United States, Pope John Paul II made a stop at Shea Stadium on October 3, 1979, as part of his seven-day tour. More than 60,000 fans flocked to Flushing to see the Pope. After having rained throughout the morning, the weather broke almost at the exact time that the Pope was due to begin his service. The tickets for the event closely resembled a ticket to a Mets game. "His Holiness Pope John Paul II at Shea" it read across the top of the ticket. There was the papal seal in the center of the ticket, with the date and the words "ticket is free of charge" on either side of the seal.

• • • •

Ten years before the Pope graced Shea Stadium, the ballpark had experienced a miracle of its own—the Miracle Mets. In the years that Shea Stadium was open—1964 through 2008—there were many, many memorable sporting events that took place. With all due respect to the Beatles, Shea was first and foremost a baseball and football stadium.

One of the most memorable games ever played at Shea was a game that many Mets fans would rather forget. On Father's Day, 1964, with the stadium not quite three months old, Philadelphia Phillies pitcher Jim Bunning pitched a perfect game against the Mets. It was somewhat appropriate for Bunning to have this perfection occur on Father's Day, as at the time he was the father of seven children. He would later go on to have a total of nine children and thirty-five grandchildren.

The Mets had plenty of great moments at Shea Stadium in its early years as well. When they clinched the National League Division Title in 1969, years of being a second-rate team at once dissolved. Leading the St. Louis Cardinals 6-0 in the bottom of the ninth inning, pitcher Gary Gentry induced first baseman Joe Torre to ground into a game-ending double play. The seemingly impossible had occurred, and Mets broadcaster Lindsay Nelson marked the occasion in style: "At 9:07 on September 24th, the Mets have won the championship of the Eastern Division of the National League."

Two weeks later, the Mets were once again on their home field when they defeated the Atlanta Braves to complete a three-game sweep and win the first-ever National League Championship Series. Ten days later, Lindsay Nelson proclaimed to everyone that the Mets were champions of the world after defeating the mighty Baltimore Orioles four games to one. It was the Mets' first championship, but it was not the first title for Shea Stadium.

One year earlier, the Jets had beaten the Mets to the punch, winning the American Football League title in front of 62,627 fans over the Oakland Raiders to advance to Super Bowl III. The Jets, greatly aware of what it meant to have a championship game on their home turf, were prepared.

Nearly one month before the game was scheduled to take place—with the Jets already having clinched the Eastern Division—ticket prices at Shea Stadium were raised for the title game. Season ticket holders were given the opportunity to purchase their usual seats for double the cost of regular-season games. There would also be approximately 2,500 standing-room-only seats that would be sold at $5 each. "Ticket orders will not be handled by mail in order to avoid theft and the Christmas Post Office rush," the *New York Times* wrote.

Whether Jets fans attending the game were sitting or standing, they definitely got their money's worth. In one of the most exciting American Football League championship games played, the Jets—led by three touchdown passes from Joe Namath—defeated the Raiders by a score of 27-23. Namath, who was referred to as the "$400,000 quarterback," lived up to all of his hype, and the Jets were headed to Super Bowl III.

No one had given the Jets much of a chance to defeat the mighty Baltimore Colts, but the final paragraph of sportswriter Dave Anderson's story in the *New York Times*, which he wrote before the game, left the door cracked open.

"Namath was injured, too," Anderson wrote, making reference to the fact that several New York Jets were banged up in the game against the Raiders. "He dislocated his left middle finger and required a Xylocaine injection on the sideline. But he doesn't pass with his left hand, as the Colts might discover to their dismay."

• • • •

Never before and never since would Shea Stadium—the multi-purpose ballpark that was realized by developer Robert Moses—be as busy as it had been for the crazy nine months of 1975. It had taken more abuse than any one stadium ever should. But it survived.

"Shea Stadium was like a home to me," said Koosman, who was on the mound when the Mets won their first world championship at Shea. "There were a lot of memories that were created there. You really got to know all of the people there and after so many years, it was like we were all family."

Jon Matlack, who pitched at Shea for the Mets from 1972 through 1977 and whose locker was located between those of Koosman and Tom Seaver, echoed his teammate's sentiments.

"Shea was a huge part of my life and will always be," Matlack said. "The fans at Shea were fantastic. If you gave them an honest effort, they really appreciated it. I had a lot of fun there with a great bunch of people."

• • • •

Thursday, June 12, 1975 was a rare off day for Shea Stadium. The turf had taken a pounding day after day, week after week, month after month, since the start of the baseball season. However, in 1975 there was no such thing as a day off for Shea Stadium.

DeWitt Clinton High School capped an undefeated baseball season by defeating Lafayette High School, 3-0, to win the Public Schools Athletic League title. DeWitt Clinton senior pitcher Rolando Acosta hurled a five-hit shutout to propel Clinton to victory. Acosta had also pitched—and won—one week earlier at Shea against Tottenville High School, advancing DeWitt Clinton to the championship game.

For Acosta, playing at Shea Stadium was truly a dream come true.

"I was awestruck, I thought I had died and went to heaven," said Acosta, thinking back fondly to his high school days. "We had a bunch of kids—mostly of color—from the South Bronx who had never been to Shea Stadium. If we had been to any stadium, it would have been to Yankee Stadium. I remember we took the bus over there, and when we got there I was just in awe. I had to keep closing my jaw, because remember we had been playing basically in sandlot facilities—nothing like a major league stadium."

Raised in the South Bronx and Washington Heights in the 1970s—after immigrating from the Domincan Republic at the age of fourteen and learning English as a second language—Acosta graduated number four in his class, out of more than one thousand students. He took his studies—and his baseball—very seriously.

"We had a great team that year and one of the things that I have always taken a lot of pride in is my ability to focus," said Acosta about not getting flustered by pitching in a major league ballpark. "The year before we had lost to Lafayette, and we wanted to win and show the world that we were the real thing. I'm glad it worked out for us."

It worked out extremely well for Acosta, who was recruited after his senior season to play baseball and attend Columbia University. There, he excelled not only on the playing field, but also in the classroom. Following graduation, he stayed right where he was, attending Columbia University Law School. Acosta would receive Columbia's "Medal for Excellence," is a member of the school's athletic hall of fame, and was awarded the Columbia Law School's 2013 Wien Prize for Social Responsibility.

Today, Acosta makes his mark not on a baseball field, but in a court of law. The Honorable Rolando T. Acosta was elected in 2002 to be a New York State Supreme Court Justice in New York County, and was appointed by New York Governor Elliot Spitzer to the Court's Appellate Division in 2008.

When he looks back at all he has accomplished—and continues to accomplish—Acosta is thrilled to think back to the time he climbed the mound at Shea Stadium.

"I would take my son to Mets games at Shea Stadium and would tell him, 'Yeah, I pitched here,' and he couldn't believe it," Acosta said, "I said, 'That's right, I did.' In some sense it's almost like a fleeting memory, but in a great sense it's like it happened yesterday. It brings you that joy. It was a lot of fun."

CHAPTER 4

Meet the Mets

ON JULY 21, THE METS played their ninetieth game of the 1975 season. Of course, Felix Millan was in the starting lineup. Millan—who was playing his third season with the Mets and tenth season overall—was always in the lineup. In fact, the steady-fielding second baseman was on his way to becoming the first New York Mets player in history to play in all one hundred and sixty-two games of a season.

On this particular day, Millan was 4-4 at the plate, singling in each of his at-bats. It was a tremendous day offensively for the native of Puerto Rico, who raised his season batting average to .297. However, despite reaching first base in four consecutive at-bats, he would never make it to second base. If that wasn't enough, Millan's success at the plate earned him only a spot in the history books, as an odd footnote in a record-setting performance by one of his teammates.

Joe Torre was not simply a good player when he was in the prime of his career—he was a great player. After spending his first eight years in the major leagues with the Braves organization—first in Milwaukee and then in Atlanta—Torre was traded to the St. Louis Cardinals for Orlando Cepeda just prior to the 1969 season.

In 1971, already a six-time all-star, Torre had a breakout season for the Cardinals. He led the National League in three top offensive categories—.363 batting average, 230 hits, and 137 runs batted in—earning the third baseman Most Valuable Player honors.

That was the high point in Torre's career, however. Following three more somewhat solid seasons in St. Louis that saw his production decline, Torre was traded to the Mets in October of 1974 for Tommy Moore and Ray Sadecki—not quite the star power of Orlando Cepeda.

"To me, this is the year that's going to let me know how much longer I can play," Torre told reporters at the time of the signing.

Heading into the game against the Houston Astros on July 21st, Torre was having a good end-of-your-career season. Entering the game with a .270 batting average, Torre could not have asked for a better table than the one Millan had set for him throughout the game. Millan singled in front of Torre all four times through the lineup.

In the bottom of the first inning, Torre was facing pitcher Ken Forsch—the brother of his former teammate Bob Forsch. With Millan on first base, Torre bounced back to the mound, allowing Forsch to start a one-four-three inning-ending double play. Oh well, no news to report, double plays happen all the time in baseball. No need to alert authorities—yet.

In the bottom of the third inning with one man out, Mets center fielder Del Unser singled, as did Millan, bringing Torre to the plate. Torre ripped a ground ball to Houston shortstop Roger Metzger, who started a six-four-three double play to end the inning. Torre was two-for-two grounding into double plays.

In the bottom of the sixth inning, Millan led off the frame with a single off of Forsch to right field. Torre followed Millan by bouncing a ball to Astros second baseman Larry Milbourne, who easily started a four-six-three double play. Torre was on the cusp of making history. Never before in its one-hundred-year history had a National League player grounded into four double plays in a single game.

Leading off the bottom of the eighth inning, Unser dragged a bunt and reached first base. Millan followed with yet another single. The way Torre's day was going, he probably would have been wise to simply drop down a sacrifice bunt and get out of Dodge. However, he hit in the three-spot, and the Mets were trailing by four runs in the game. Besides, no one had grounded into four double plays in a game in a hundred years. Torre changed all of that with one swing of the bat, grounding once again to the shortstop, who once again started a six-four-three double play. It was time to alert the authorities.

"I'd like to thank Felix Millan for making all of this possible," Torre said, tongue in cheek, to reporters after the game. "He ought to get an assist."

When questioned about his approach at the plate in the bottom of the eighth inning, Torre insisted that he didn't waver.

"I wasn't worried. I wasn't anxious," he said. "I made up my mind to be aggressive."

For Millan's part, he was still laughing about Torre's performance—and postgame comments about it being Millan's fault—four decades later when he was interviewed by the New York *Daily News*.

"He could've hit a home run or something, couldn't he?" Millan joked.

• • • •

When the New York Mets made their appearance on the major league scene, the new ballpark that they would call home was not yet complete. There were a number of delays—weather and otherwise—causing the opening of the new stadium in Flushing, Queens, to be pushed off until the 1964 season. That meant the Mets would have to play their first two seasons in the dilapidated old Polo Grounds.

So for the 1962 and 1963 seasons—the Mets' initial two seasons in baseball—the team reluctantly played at the Polo Grounds. It wasn't a pretty sight, for the team or the stadium. By 1962, the Polo Grounds—which opened in 1911—was considerably past its prime. The locker rooms were cramped, the concession stands were outdated, and the stadium had not had any real maintenance done—aside from a few coats of blue and orange paint—since the Giants headed west.

The New York Titans football team of the American Football League had been playing at the Polo Grounds since the team was founded in 1960. However, other than those seven games per season, the old stadium in Manhattan had been completely empty since the end of the 1957 season.

"They made it so we could play in it," said Ed Kranepool, who started opening day in 1962 with the Mets as a seventeen-year-old. "It was painted, but it was dark. The clubhouse was terrible, and the conditions there were strange. It wasn't easy to get to. We were looking forward to moving into Shea."

The team's play was not much better than the condition of the stadium it played in. The 1962 Mets lost 120 of their 160 games, a record of ineptness that still stands. The team did not fare much better in year two at the Polo Grounds, as New York lost 111 games. It had to be the building, right? After all, the manager of the Mets was the mighty Casey Stengel—who had led the New York Yankees to seven world championships. Of course, by 1962 Stengel was more grandfatherly than mighty and the Mets did not have Mantle or DiMaggio. Things would have to improve at Shea Stadium.

When Shea opened its doors in 1964, the Mets—and all of baseball—were ready to see how things would change for the young National League team in New York. They didn't, really.

The 1964 Mets drew 1,732,597 fans to their new ballpark—second most in the National League—but did not win too many more games, posting a 53-109 record. The highlight of the first season at Shea was hosting the Major League Baseball All-Star Game in July. That game was even more memorable for the Mets, as their second baseman Ron Hunt was named as a starter—the first-ever Mets all-star.

The Mets did not have a winning season through their first seven seasons, finishing ninth or tenth—dead last—in the National League every year. That all changed in 1969—thanks for the most part to a young pitcher by the name of George Thomas Seaver. It was in that season that the right-hander truly earned his nickname, "The Franchise."

Tom Seaver was the Mets' ace and in 1975 he showed why, winning twenty-two games and his third Cy Young Award. *Photo courtesy of the National Baseball Hall of Fame*

After back-to-back sixteen-win seasons in 1967 and 1968, Seaver won a National League-best twenty-five games, including eighteen complete games in 1969. However, that season Seaver did much more than compile tremendous statistics and earn his first Cy Young—he also changed the image of the loveable-loser Mets. Many believe that the Mets' coronation began when they shocked the world by winning the 1969 World Series. In reality, it happened much earlier that summer.

On July 9, the Mets were facing the first-place Chicago Cubs, sending thirteen-game winner Tom Seaver to the mound against Chicago's Ken Holtzman. Seaver was flawless during the game, mowing down Cub after Cub, and taking a perfect game into the ninth inning. However, it was what happened in the bottom of the eighth inning that changed everything for many Mets fans, including current Mets broadcaster and unofficial team historian, Howie Rose.

"I am fortunate enough to have been at Shea Stadium to see the Mets win the division, the pennant and the World Series, but my most memorable night in that ballpark was July 9, 1969," Rose said. "It was the first big series that the Mets had ever played with pennant implications and the build-up to it was just enormous. If there is any one moment I relish from all the years at Shea Stadium it was the ovation—and I can put myself into the story—that *we* gave Tom when he came to bat in the bottom of the eighth inning. It was the most thunderous, meaningful ovation I'd ever heard or taken part in in my life. It wasn't just that he had a perfect game going. As he walked from the on-deck circle to home plate, the cheers and the ovation had as much to do with the realization that the Mets had arrived, that this was not only a good young pitcher, but a transcendent player, and he was ours. If we were going to get there, he was going to be the guy to get us there."

Jerry Koosman will go down in history as one of the greatest pitchers the Mets have ever had, winning sixty-three games over four seasons in the mid-1970s. *Photo courtesy of the National Baseball Hall of Fame*

With one out in the bottom of the ninth inning, Jim Qualls spoiled Seaver's bid for perfection, but nothing could diminish what Seaver accomplished that night—both on the field and in the hearts and minds of Mets fans.

"When you realize for the first time that the joke's over, that's a very, very profound feeling and that was all encapsulated in that ovation," Rose recalled. "Being a part of that—and what it meant—is my single greatest memory in that ballpark. That was the night the Mets grew up."

The Mets rode that wave all the way to a division title, the National League pennant, and then into the 1969 World Series against the heavily favored Baltimore Orioles.

After losing the first game to the Orioles in Baltimore, the Mets captured the next three games, giving them the chance to clinch their first world championship at home in Shea Stadium. To a man, the Mets players knew that it was critical that they close out the World Series in Game Five at Shea Stadium.

"We all certainly had high hopes that we would win that last game at home because we didn't want to go back to Baltimore," said Mets second-year pitcher Jerry Koosman, who along with Seaver provided the Mets with perhaps the best one-two punch in all of baseball. "There was a lot of emphasis put on that."

Seaver's excellence in 1969 somewhat overshadowed the terrific season that Koosman had, winning seventeen games, including sixteen complete games, and compiling an earned run average of 2.67. One year earlier, as a rookie, Koosman had won nineteen games, been selected to the All-Star Game, and finished behind Johnny Bench by a single vote for National League Rookie of the Year honors. Koosman, in reality, was not a two in a one-two punch—he was a 1A.

"We had a really good relationship," Koosman said of Seaver. "We relied on each other's help in terms of mechanics and I kept all of his pitching charts because I was always pitching after him. We had a great rapport with all of our pitchers. We were very competitive with each other and I think that helped a lot as far as our success is concerned."

So it was Koosman, who had won Game Two of the 1969 World Series in Baltimore, who was on the mound in the potential clinching game back at Shea Stadium. Things looked a little less optimistic when the Mets found themselves trailing early in the game.

"Certainly there's a lot of pressure on you and we fell behind early 3-0, but I only gave up one hit for the rest of the game," Koosman said. "I can remember it very clearly. I was very nervous. I didn't have control over my curveball, but I had a lot of energy. My fastball was excellent."

By the time the ninth inning came around, the packed house at Shea Stadium was in a frenzy. In fact, it was because of that crowd noise that Koosman wasn't sure if a two-out fly ball was going to stay in the big stadium and give the Mets their first title.

"The crowd was so loud that you couldn't hear the ball hit the bat," Koosman remembered. "So when Davey Johnson hit my fastball to left field to Cleon Jones, I didn't hear it hit the bat. When you don't hear it hit the bat, it's tough to tell how far the ball is going to go because the sound of the ball leaving the bat coordinates with the flight of the ball. So I was kind of nervous at first when the ball flew into left field."

It didn't take Koosman long to exhale, however.

"I really had to look at Cleon to see his reaction to it," he said. "When I saw him go back, just about to the warning track and then stop, I knew that the ball was in the ballpark."

It capped a great year for Koosman and the Mets.

"Certainly 1969 sticks out as tops," Koosman said. "The ticker-tape parade was great. There were a lot of special moments, but the top ones were no doubt in 1969."

• • • •

Early on in 1975, the Mets were a confident bunch, two years removed from the National League pennant and one year removed from a horrific fall from the top. While the Mets' new tenants—the Yankees—were enjoying success in 1974, Yogi Berra's Mets slipped from number one in the National League to a fifth-place finish in the National League East—finishing twenty games under the .500 mark.

The Yankees entered the 1975 season—their final season at Shea—with high expectations, and the arrival of big-name players such as Catfish Hunter and Bobby Bonds. The Mets also had some new faces at the start of the season, although Torre and slugger Dave Kingman—who like Bonds played for San Francisco in 1974—did not inspire Mets fans with the same exuberance that Yankees fans might have been feeling.

Still, the Mets were full of veterans, such as Torre, Kingman, Seaver, Koosman, and Rusty Staub. Two months into the 1975 season, the Mets were keeping their heads above water and the players were preaching patience.

"I wasn't here in '69, but in '73 we didn't have any togetherness until late in the season," Staub said early into the 1975 season. "This year, we've got it early. We've also got a stronger bench and several new faces—Joe Torre, Del Unser, and imagine getting Dave Kingman for money. That's a gift from the gods."

The Mets players weren't the only ones with of confident approach.

"It might be the best baseball summer in New York in two decades," sports columnist Dave Anderson wrote in the *New York Times*. "Both the Mets and the Yankees are not only winning, but they also look as if they'll keep winning; they've never done that before, at least not together."

Anderson was almost willing the teams to play well, as a means to an end for residents of New York City, who sat helpless as their city plunged deeper and deeper into financial despair.

"More than ever, New York needs good baseball now—for the morale of its citizens," Anderson wrote. "If not for the taxes from the Shea Stadium tenants for its treasury. When the city's treasury isn't over .500, its ball clubs better be."

Tom Seaver was not having a problem staying above .500 in 1975. After a very average, back-aching season in 1974, Seaver returned to his superstar form. It soon became extremely clear that Tom Terrific's 11-11 campaign in 1974 was simply an aberration. Since arriving in the major leagues with the Mets in 1967, Seaver had been selected to the All-Star Game every season and earned the

Cy Young Award twice. So for Seaver, struggling through 1974 was uncharted territory.

"It was very frustrating," Seaver told the *New York Times* following the 1974 season. "I didn't go around beating my wife or anything, but I was grouchy. It entered my mind, either you pitch effectively, or you don't have a job. . . . The trouble goes back to the year before last; I ended the 1973 season with a sore shoulder, then went into spring training last year trying to protect my arm. So I got lazy with the mechanics of pitching."

Prior to the start of the 1975 campaign, the Mets ace agreed to take the maximum cut in salary allowed by rule. Today, the thought of anyone—let alone the star of your team—taking a pay cut for a poor season is implausible. But in the 1970s, it was business as usual.

"I wasn't disturbed that I got a cut after one bad year," Seaver told reporters prior to the start of the season. "The ball club's been very good and honest with me, and I with them. They paid me a good amount of money last year and I didn't pitch up to that amount."

Seaver's pay cut amounted to $34,000 and dropped him from the lofty status of being the highest-paid pitcher in baseball history at that point. That honor now went to Seaver's fellow Shea Stadium pitcher—Catfish Hunter of the Yankees—who signed to pitch for $150,000 per season. Seaver was quick to point out that he and Hunter were not rivals, but instead were colleagues.

"My primary motive in pitching is not to outdo Catfish Hunter," Seaver said. "I'm all for him. Anytime you have somebody who gets money like that, he raises salaries below him."

In addition to the Mets' decision to lower Seaver's salary, they also decided to raise ticket prices in 1975 for box seats—from four dollars to four dollars and fifty cents. The Mets' made out both ways, as Seaver was on point throughout the season and fans came out in droves to watch him pitch.

Seaver starting quickly in 1975 by outdueling Philadelphia Phillies lefty ace Steve Carlton on Opening Day. Seaver scattered six hits and gave up just one earned run, striking out nine Phillies. The Mets finished off their first win in style when one of their newest faces, Joe Torre, ripped a run-scoring single to left field against Carlton in the bottom of the ninth inning. One game, one walk-off victory—not a bad start to the season.

Seaver struggled throughout his first nine decisions, compiling a record of five wins and four losses. He then kicked things into another gear, winning fifteen of his next eighteen games. The fifteenth win of that string was his twentieth victory of the season, a 3-0 decision over the Pittsburgh Pirates. In that game, Seaver gave up just four hits and struck out ten Pirates, raising the Mets to eight games above the .500 mark with a record of 72-64.

The Mets ace would finish the 1975 season with a record of twenty-two wins—tops in the National League—and a league-best 234 strikeouts. Seaver's bounce-back season earned him his third Cy Young Award.

"Seaver was the best," said Ed Kranepool, who had been Seaver's teammate since 1967. "You gave him the ball and you knew you were going to get eight innings out of him. Same with Koosman. Both great pitchers, there's no question about it."

Jerry Koosman actually finished third in the Mets' victory total in 1975, winning fourteen games against thirteen losses. It was Jon Matlack—pitching behind Seaver and Koosman—who was able to win sixteen games. Matlack was no stranger to success, however. The left-handed pitcher was named the National League Rookie of the Year in 1972, four years after Seaver won the same award and three years after Koosman finished just behind Johnny Bench in the voting.

One of the highlights of Matlack's season in 1975 was being named to the All-Star team, pitching in the game, getting the win over—of all people, Catfish Hunter—and being named as the game's co-Most Valuable Player. He shared that honor with Bill Madlock of the Cubs.

"It was an exciting time and a very special honor to be involved in that game," said Matlack, who recounted how his All-Star performance was almost not to be.

With the National League leading 3-0, and Matlack's teammate Tom Seaver on the mound, Boston's Carl Yastrzemski sent a long blast to right-center field, where Matlack was warming up in the bullpen.

"I was in the bullpen getting myself loosened up and ready and starting to do my warm-up throws," Matlack remembered. "The home run damn near hit me in the head as I was warming up. I heard the bat crack and the guys in the bullpen started yelling 'watch out, watch out' and the ball came flying in."

Fortunately, the ball eluded Matlack. However, would he have blamed Seaver had he gotten plunked?

"I would have blamed him any chance I could," said Matlack, laughing heartily.

Throughout the mid-1970s, the Matlack-Seaver-Koosman trio was as formidable a pitching rotation as there was in all of baseball.

"It was the best of all worlds," Matlack said. "Fortunately, my locker was placed right between Seaver and Koosman. There was a wrought-iron beam between Tommy and me, but Koosy and I were right next to each other and I couldn't have been in better hands. I got information from two very skilled technicians that helped me along my way. It was a great environment to play in and a great environment to pitch in."

When Matlack came up and joined the rotation in 1972, Seaver and Koosman were already established as championship pitchers. It was something that Matlack was honored to be a part of, if not a little overwhelmed.

"It was sort of a daunting honor," said Matlack of his first season with the Mets, and his early success. "At one point I picked up the *New York Times*, which would list the league leaders in the sports section. There at the top of the National League pitching was Jon Matlack, 6-0. I was flabbergasted and said to myself 'What the hell are you doing there?'"

However, instead of embracing his early success, Matlack pushed it away as if he didn't deserve it, questioning himself and his skills. That was quickly put to rest by the Mets' ace.

"Before I could blink I tried to give it away," Matlack said. "It was like I wasn't comfortable doing as well as I was doing. Seaver grabbed me at one point shortly thereafter and said, 'Look, if you don't own the success that you have, you're doomed to give it back. You're entitled to it because you worked your tail off to get here. You have to own it, put it in your pocket, and keep it with you, or you're going to give it back.' It was some of the greatest advice I had ever received."

One of the most important story lines regarding the Mets pitching staff in 1975, however, was who was *not* a part of it. Prior to the start of the season, the Mets traded away one of their most popular and emotional pitchers when they sent Tug McGraw to the Philadelphia Phillies. McGraw had been the Mets' top reliever in 1972 and 1973, saving twenty-seven and twenty-five games respectively.

During the Mets' bizarre run to the National League pennant in 1973—finishing just three games above .500—McGraw sparked the Mets to the finish line with his "Ya Gotta Believe" charge. He was a fan favorite, for sure. However, McGraw dealt with injuries for much of the 1974 season and the Mets decided to unload their closer. At the time of his trade, he was the Mets' franchise leader in saves, games pitched, and games finished.

"The trade really hurt me at the time," McGraw wrote in his autobiography. "I'd been with the Mets from the start, and I thought I'd always be a Met. The Mets were my baseball family. I'd had a taste of the spotlight in New York, and I loved it. I didn't want to leave."

When the Phillies made the trip to open the 1975 season at Shea Stadium, McGraw was on the disabled list. By league rule, McGraw would only be allowed to sit in the dugout with permission from the opposing manager—in this case, the Mets' Yogi Berra.

"I'll let him stay," Yogi said, in typical Yogi fashion, "if he keeps quiet."

• • • •

While McGraw was saddened to be traded away from New York, slugger Dave Kingman was overjoyed to be heading to the Big Apple in 1975. The Mets paid the San Francisco Giants $150,000 for the six-foot-six home run specialist known as King Kong. Four years earlier,

Kong slammed a home run that smashed off the windshield of the Giants' team bus, parked behind the left field bullpen. Kingman was thrilled with his relocation.

"You can't come to a better place than Shea Stadium," Kingman said during a television interview in 1975. "It's a great ballpark and a great town. The fans are the greatest fans around, and playing in New York has been one of the greatest thrills that I have had."

The Mets got their money's worth, as Kingman set a team record with thirty-six home runs and led the team with twenty game-winning hits.

Kingman was an all-or-nothing hitter, however, as many home run hitters are known to be. He would hit home runs in bunches and then strike out in just as many bunches. He quickly became known as a feast or famine offensive force for the Mets.

"It was all or nothing from a fielding perspective too," Matlack said of Kingman, laughing during an interview in 2013. "Every time he played right field and the ball went in that direction, I held my breath until it went into his glove."

Along with Kingman, Rusty Staub had a record-setting season at the plate. Now in his fourth season with the Mets, Staub was the team's best hitter. The right fielder batted close to .300 for much of the season, finishing the year with a .282 average. However, it was Staub's clutch hitting that set him apart. For the first time in his thirteen-year career—and the first time in the Mets' thirteen-year history—Staub drove in more than one hundred runs, finishing 1975 with 105 runs batted in. He also had thirty doubles and nineteen homers, which garnered him several votes in the Most Valuable Player voting at the end of the season.

The Mets rewarded Staub for his offensive prowess by trading him to the Detroit Tigers following the season. The Mets received an over-the-hill Mickey Lolich and two other players for Staub, who went on to continue his strong offensive play. Today, the trade is regarded as one of the worst in franchise history.

• • • •

After being named the American League's Manager of the Year in 1974, the Yankees' Bill Virdon did not make it through the entire 1975 campaign.
Photo courtesy of the National Baseball Hall of Fame

The Mets and Yankees had much more in common in 1975 than sharing Shea Stadium. Each team had arguably the best pitcher in its league—Seaver with the Mets and Hunter with the Yankees; each team imported a slugger during the off-season—Kingman with the Mets and Bonds with the Yankees; each team had a sixteen-game winner—Matlack with the Mets and Doc Medich with the Yankees; and each team had a fourteen-game winner—Koosman with the Mets and Rudy May with the Yankees.

All of these similarities probably made Mets manager Yogi Berra more than a little nervous when the Yankees decided to fire their manager, Bill Virdon. As it turned out, Virdon's fate was sealed on July 20, when the Texas Rangers fired Martin as their manager. From that moment on, Yankees owner George Steinbrenner was on the hunt—he wanted Martin to lead his team. So when Virdon was finally fired, it was not a total surprise.

Berra's fate—it turns out—was actually sealed two days before Virdon's, when he had a run-in with one of his players, veteran Cleon Jones. Jones had already had serious issues with the front office earlier in the season, after an incident that occurred in Florida during spring training. Jones was arrested for indecent exposure after being found in the back of a van with a woman who was not his wife. Jones was never prosecuted, but the Mets fined him heavily and forced him to hold a press conference and apologize. Jones was incensed, and everything came to a head on July 18.

After pinch-hitting late in the game against the Atlanta Braves, Jones refused to go out and play in the field. Berra ordered him to go into the game and the two ended up having a shouting match, which included Jones throwing his glove and other objects in the dugout. Berra was quoted at the time in the *Sporting News* as saying it was "the most embarrassing thing that has happened to me since I became a manager."

It was not the first time Jones was surrounded by controversy. In 1969, two and a half months before Koosman watched the final out of the Amazin' World Series drop into Jones's glove, there was a real concern whether Jones would still be on the squad come October.

On July 30, 1969, Jones—who was an all-star that season—was the leading hitter in the National League with a batting average of .346. The Mets were taking on the Houston Astros in a doubleheader at Shea and from its earliest stages, it was a miserable day for the New Yorkers. Playing on a rain-soaked field, the Mets lost the first game to the Astros, 16-3. However, it was in the second game that the real problem started. With the Mets already trailing 7-0 in the bottom of the third inning, Houston's Johnny Edwards doubled to left field. Jones—who had been nursing a leg injury, but insisted he was fit to play—retrieved the ball and threw it back to the infield. Mets manager Gil Hodges popped out of the dugout.

Hodges was as tough as nails when it came to player discipline, but his players loved him. So did the New York fans, who remembered him as a beloved player for the Brooklyn Dodgers two decades earlier.

There was no love on Hodges's mind as he slowly walked out of the dugout. Jones would later state he thought his manager was coming out to make a pitching change, slowly walking toward the mound. But Hodges continued past the mound, toward the shortstop. Bud Harrelson made eye contact with his manager and gestured—not all that visibly—wondering if it was him who was about to catch Hodges's ire. The Mets' manager tilted his head "no" to Harrelson and continued walking.

When he reached his left fielder, Hodges supposedly asked Jones if he was healthy enough to play and why he didn't hustle for the ball. He mentioned he didn't like the way Jones went after the ball. Clearly, he said some combination of these things, as the exact conversation was relayed to people differently. In any event, whatever explanation Jones gave Hodges, the manager was not pleased with it.

Hodges turned and walked back to the dugout, with Jones trailing him, head slumped down. In later years, Jones would call this one of the most important points of his career and say that Hodges was the best manager he ever had. It was clear to everyone at that moment that Hodges would never settle for less than 100 percent.

Following that night, the Mets went on to win forty-five of their final sixty-four games, winning the division, the pennant, and completing the season with that fly ball settling into the mitt of Jones.

Six years later, it wasn't that Jones was *pulled* from left field—it was that he refused to *go* to left field. Once again this was an important moment in Jones's career, but this time, it would not lead to a championship for him or his team.

Berra took a hard-line stance with Jones and with upper management, insisting it was "him or me." Mets chairman M. Donald Grant was not all that pleased with Berra's public stance, as he didn't want the situation to blow up into a bigger issue than it was—specifically when it came to race relations. The *New York Times* reported that Grant "felt vibrations that some persons in the black community resented the club's handling of Jones through his ten-year career." Still, after the Mets tried their best to trade Jones, he was released on July 27.

Berra had seemingly won the battle, but as he would find out just a week after his counterpart with the Yankees was fired, he would lose the war. Berra was fired by the Mets on August 8 and replaced by former Mets infielder Roy McMillan.

Grant insisted that Berra's firing was more about wins and losses than with Cleon Jones.

"It's been a decision that has been going through our heads for some time," Grant said of his former manager, who took over in April of 1972 when Hodges died suddenly of a heart attack. "It had nothing to do with failing attendance, dissension on the team, the recent increasingly turbulent problem we had over Cleon Jones, or the Yankees' change in managers. Nothing had anything to do it with it but the performance of the team."

In reality, all of the things Grant mentioned had most likely played a role in Berra's firing. Dissension had been lurking about for a long time. The day Berra was let go, several players made their feelings known.

"It was obvious that things were being wasted," said Jon Matlack, who had at times expressed criticism of his manager following games. "They were being wasted either because we weren't playing up to our capabilities, or because he wasn't managing up to his."

"Yogi was making moves that didn't sit well with the team," said Jerry Koosman. "If somebody made a mental error . . . Yogi would say, 'Next time it's gonna cost ya.' And it became a saying, 'Next time it's gonna cost ya.' And you'd get away with it over and over."

Everyone was looking to Seaver for a comment after Berra's firing, and after at first declining, he did in fact speak with reporters, saying he had expected this move for some time.

"There's a different man managing," said Seaver, referring to his new skipper, McMillan. "I'm sure things will be different . . . different in a very positive way."

For his part, Berra had nothing negative to say about the Mets or his firing. Always a gentleman of the game, Yogi admitted that following a doubleheader loss the night before, he was prepared for the worst.

"I had an inkling this was going to happen," Berra said. "It comes with the game. You're hired to be fired. But I'm not sad. What's to be sad about?

"Maybe that's the way I'm made," Berra continued. "I did my best and I wouldn't do anything differently. I felt the same way when I was hitting. I'd say 'I'm not up there to make an out.' Now I've got two acres of land and a fifteen-room house that I never thought I'd have when I started out. I never thought I'd be in the Hall of Fame, either."

While Yogi himself would not point any fingers, plenty of members of the media and his friends throughout baseball stood up for him.

"Make no mistake about it, Yogi Berra was not dismissed as manager of the New York Mets because the team skidded into a five-game losing streak. That would be like saying Richard M. Nixon resigned as President a year ago because our balance of payments was a little low that month," sportswriter Joseph Durso wrote in the *New York Times*. "The gun was already pointed at Yogi's head when the chairman of the board of directors, M. Donald Grant, pulled the trigger. And the stage was set for the execution when Yogi stood up to his boss on the tricky issue of Cleon Jones."

One of the greatest sportswriters of all time, Red Smith, focused much of his post-firing column on Yogi Berra, the man.

"Yogi is a low-keyed leader," Smith wrote. "He has a naturally sweet disposition, seldom gets excited and rarely loses his temper. If he ever put his foot down with the Mets, he was careful to remove his spikes first."

Smith continued that while Jones earned his release from the Mets, allowed to now sell his services to any other team, Berra was just plain out of work.

"Somebody had to be the fall guy," Smith wrote. "Chairmen of the board rarely ever are."

• • • •

The late Montreal Expos manager Gene Mauch might have summed up the firing of Yogi Berra best.

"It's a shame a man like Yogi Berra is fired because of recalcitrant players."

However, it was Mauch's Expos that helped push Berra out the back door of Shea Stadium.

The official stance from the Mets front office was that Berra was not fired because of any one thing—such as unhappy player(s)—but in fact because it was the right time for him to make a change for the underperforming team. If Grant and the Mets' front office were look-ing for an exclamation mark for that sentence, they certainly got it on August 4, when the Mets hosted Mauch's Expos.

Longtime minor league pitcher Randy Tate was on the mound for the Mets. Tate had been unspectacular for the Mets throughout his rookie season and entered the game with four wins and nine losses. On this particular night, though, Tate had it all working. He was striking out hitters at a record pace and other than a walk here and there, didn't allow any base runners. In fact, Tate no-hit the Expos through the first seven innings and took a 3-0 lead into the eighth inning.

In the top of the eighth inning, with one out and one on—via a walk—Tate struck out Jim Dwyer for his thirteenth strikeout of the game—a career high. After pinch-hitter Jim Lyttle singled to left field, breaking up the no-hitter, Tate walked the next batter, Pepe Mangual. That brought a rookie catcher by the name of Gary Carter to the plate at Shea, who promptly drove a single to left, scoring Lyttle to break up Tate's shutout.

With the no-hitter and shutout gone, it seemed to be a given that Berra would go to his bullpen and bring in one of his relievers. After all, Tate was not Seaver or Koosman or Matlack. There was no pedigree there, where Berra could say, "I've seen Tate get out of these messes." The fact was, he never had. It was one thing to keep Tate in to attempt to get his no-hitter, but following the hit—and most certainly following the walk—it was another scenario entirely. Even if Berra could justify leaving Tate in for those two hitters, there was no rational explanation for Tate to still be in the game against Carter. Upstairs, Grant must have been fuming.

Following Carter's hit, former and future Met Mike Jorgensen stepped up to the plate and ripped Tate's heart—and Berra's job—over the right-center-field fence. Suddenly, in a flash, the Mets were trailing 4-3. They would lose the game by that score and Tate fell to 4-10 on the year. He would pitch a couple more games for the Mets in 1975 and then never appear in the majors again.

Twenty-four hours later—following the doubleheader sweep at the hands of those same Expos—Yogi was out of a job. Unlike Tate, however, Berra—already a Hall of Famer—would make it back to the big leagues.

• • • •

The man who Berra played for during most of his career—Casey Stengel—returned to Shea Stadium in all of his glory for the 1975 Old-Timers Day on June 28th. Stengel had managed the Mets for the franchise's first three seasons, playing the dual role of skipper and loveable patriarch for the fledgling ball club. Mets fans had nothing but high praise for the man known as the Ol' Professor and were thrilled to see him ten years later.

Stengel arrived in style, wearing a gladiator helmet and riding in a chariot drawn by two white horses. He later walked across the field, arm in arm with Mets owner Joan Whitey Payson. The duo was in many ways once the parents—now, maybe the grandparents—of the Mets. Payson was still the president of the team in name, but was not involved in day-to-day details. As the elderly couple cruised through the outfield, legends such as Joe DiMaggio, Willie Mays, and Ralph Kiner could only stand and smile. Their smiles, however, paled in comparison to the old man himself, who was grinning from ear to ear, waving to the Shea Stadium crowd—his crowd—in his city. Stengel and Payson were waving to the crowd as if it was the last time either would have the opportunity to do so. It turned out it was.

During the two-inning Old-Timers game itself, Mays and Kiner each had base hits, although the American League bested the National League oldies, by a score of 6-2. Not that anyone really cared about the outcome of that game. The one that was played for real later in the afternoon—following a massive rainstorm—saw the Mets defeat Steve Carlton and the Philadelphia Phillies by a final score of 5-2.

Almost exactly three months later, on September 29—one day after the 1975 baseball season ended—Stengel died. For very different reasons, Stengel had been equally important to both the Mets and Yankees franchises. He had guided the ultra-talented Yankees of the 1950s to seven world championships. By 1962, he was the perfect person to cast as the lovable, grandfather-type skipper to lead the infant Mets. His uniform number thirty-seven is retired by both teams.

Just five days later, Payson—the woman who hired Stengel in 1962 and paraded through the outfield with him just months earlier—also

Ed Kranepool made his Mets debut straight out of high school in 1962. By the time 1975 rolled around, Kranepool was a thirteen-year veteran at the age of thirty. *Photo courtesy of the National Baseball Hall of Fame*

died. In a matter of days, the New York Mets had lost two of the biggest figures from the franchise's start—their original heart and soul.

Payson had inherited more than a hundred million dollars in the 1920s and was always a familiar figure sitting in her front-row box at Shea Stadium. She devoted her life to civic causes, her racing stables, and her beloved Mets. When she financed the National League expansion team, she originally wanted to name it the New York Meadowlarks, but was persuaded to go with the Metropolitans. She was the first woman to buy majority control of a team in a major North American sports league.

• • • •

On Saturday, September 20, 1975, the Mets played what would be their final home victory of the season against Philadelphia in front of just 18,863 faithful at Shea. The Mets were long out of the pennant race, and were playing out the string. Their field had been battered and broken, and—in one case—almost blown up. Still, the Mets had a few more fireworks of their own for their fans.

To start, it was not a good day for starters. The Mets' Koosman lasted just three innings, giving up four earned runs and six hits. The Phillies' Wayne Simpson had an even shorter stay, giving up three earned runs in an inning and two thirds.

After three innings, the Mets jumped out to a 6-4 lead—a lead that they extended to 7-5 heading to the ninth inning. However, the Mets were not about to make things easy on their fans—or themselves.

In the top of the ninth inning, the Phillies manufactured two runs against Mets reliever Rick Baldwin, to tie the game at 7-7. That score remained until the bottom of the eleventh inning when with two outs and nobody on, Ed Kranepool singled to center field. Kranepool had been a catalyst for the Mets since joining the team in 1962 as a seventeen-year-old kid out of James Monroe High School in the Bronx.

"I started my career when I was seventeen. I was playing against Hall of Famers, batting cleanup when I was seventeen. Now that was pressure," Kranepool said. "They talk about pressure today, but today some players don't break in until they are twenty-five. I was a kid grow-ing up in the major leagues, which was very difficult to do."

Kranepool had enjoyed a very solid season in 1975, batting .322 while playing mostly first base. This had been yet another lost season for Kranepool's team, a reality he was going to have to endure for the remainder of his career.

But today, here he was, standing on first base as the winning run, as catcher Ron Hodges stepped up to the plate. Hodges was not really a home run threat at the plate, having hit only one homer in all of 1975. In fact, he had only six home runs during his career up until this moment. So when Hodges blasted a two-run, game-winning home run, the fans that remained at Shea Stadium exploded in joy.

It would be the final cheers for the Mets at Shea in 1975. The next day they lost to the Phillies and headed out for a six-game road trip to close out the season. It would be the Yankees who would be playing out the final week of the season at Shea Stadium.

• • • •

One of the games on that road trip was almost historic. Nearly two months after Randy Tate's near-no-hitter, Tom Seaver took another crack at being the first Mets pitcher to accomplish the feat. Like his bid in 1969, Seaver was pitching once again against the Chicago Cubs—although this time at Wrigley Field.

The Mets' ace was absolutely perfect through six innings, retiring the first eighteen Cubs who came to bat. In the bottom of the seventh inning, Seaver walked Chicago shortstop Don Kessinger to lead off the frame. After a sacrifice bunt, groundout, and intentional walk, Seaver struck out first baseman Andre Thornton looking to end the inning with his no-hitter intact.

In the bottom of the eighth inning, Seaver had little trouble retir-ing the Cubs, getting two fly-ball outs and a groundout. There was one very glaring problem, however. The Mets offense had not managed to score against Chicago pitcher Rick Reuschel, who had a shutout of his own on the line.

After Reuschel retired the Mets in order in the top of the ninth, Seaver headed to the mound knowing that a nine-inning no-hitter would not be enough to celebrate. Perhaps that reality affected Seaver, who—after striking out the first two hitters in the bottom of the ninth—surrendered a single to right field to Joe Wallis. Seaver got out of the ninth by striking out Thornton looking once again, but the no-hitter was history. Seaver went back out in the bottom of the tenth of the still-scoreless game and gave up a couple of more hits—but no runs.

Finally, in the bottom of the eleventh inning, with Mets reliever Skip Lockwood now on the mound, the Mets were put out of their misery—but in the worst of ways. After Lockwood gave up a leadoff single to Rick Monday, he walked Wallis. Following a sacrifice, the Mets intentionally walked Thornton to load the bases, setting up a force at home, as well as a double play. It didn't seem like the prudent move, being that the batter coming to the plate was Chicago third baseman Bill Madlock—who was hitting .360 on the season—the best in the National League.

Fortunately for the Mets, Madlock never made contact. Unfortunately for the Mets, he didn't have to. Lockwood walked the slugger to force in the game-winning run. It was just another tough loss and another near-miss for a Mets pitcher attempting to pitch a no-hitter.

Four days later, Seaver started—and won—the Mets' final game of the 1975 season in Philadelphia.

The Mets followed up the season-ending victory by heading to Shea Stadium one last time—to clean out their lockers.

CHAPTER 5

New York State of Mind

WHILE SHEA STADIUM WAS THE epicenter for the Mets, Yankees, Giants, and Jets in 1975, the city itself became a main focal point when it came to sports, politics, and pop culture.

It's hard to picture what New York City was like in the 1970s if you didn't live through it. The New York City of today hardly resembles the dirty, broken down—and just plain broke—city of 1975. The subways were dirty, dangerous, and full of graffiti. New York City's buses were not much better.

One of the many areas to avoid in New York City was the Bowery, which is on the lower east side of southern Manhattan and was sort of a skid row. The expression Bowery Bums aptly described the people living on the streets—not to be confused with the Brooklyn Bums, who had played baseball over at Ebbets Field. In the 1970s, the Bowery and many other areas, including Times Square, were known for prostitution, illicit activities, and drug dealers. The combination of New York City being out of money and many New Yorkers dealing with hard times was enough to send the city into a terrible downspin.

Throughout 1975, New York City would scramble not to fall into bankruptcy, pulling money from place to place and eliminating many social and municipal services. Just a few months into the year, banks—already wary that the mayor could not cut spending and attempt to balance the budget—would cut off credit to the city. It was very obvious that New York City could not pay off what it owed and, in many cases, cover its payroll.

New York City suffered devastating consequences. Over the next three years, more than six thousand teachers' jobs would be cut, as would more than six thousand police officer jobs. More than two thousand firefighters also would lose their jobs. Mayor Abe Beame and New York State Governor Hugh Carey first went to Washington, D.C., to ask President Ford for help in mid-May of 1975.

The day after meeting with the president, however, Beame and Carey were told to do the best they could with what they had. Some of President Ford's advisors were not nearly as diplomatic. Ford's chief of staff, Donald Rumsfeld, said that New York City's request for help was "outrageous" and that giving that help would be "a disaster."

New York City would have to endure six more months waving in the wind before President Ford provided any help at all. In fact, the president was having his own issues in 1975—his first full year in office after the resignation of Richard Nixon.

• • • •

August 8, 1974, was a rare off day at Shea Stadium during the first summer the Yankees and Mets were sharing the big ballpark. It was probably for the best. There were other things on the minds of New Yorkers and all Americans, for that matter.

Nixon's resignation came just after 9 p.m., a little over two years after burglars had broken into the Democratic National Headquarters at the Watergate Office Complex in Washington, DC. For more than two years, the American public learned more and more about the case and about Nixon's involvement.

"At the beginning, the idea of the president ordering guys to go into the campaign headquarters of the Democratic Party seemed unlikely," said Carl Stern, the award-winning NBC News correspondent, who covered Washington, DC, in the 1970s. "Eventually, it reached a tipping point where you realized that the president has to be in here somewhere. It was not instant. It came at the end of a long line of incriminating developments."

Stern was no stranger to covering Washington, having broken the story on the FBI's illegal surveillance on people and groups throughout the nation. Stern—who is an attorney—was the perfect person for NBC News to have on the ground as the Nixon fiasco unfolded.

"Legally, it played out the way it should have, the system worked," Stern said. "There was no rush to judgment. Up until the very end, there was a substantial body of public opinion that this was all—as [White House Press Secretary] Ron Ziegler called it—a 'second-rate burglary' and 'not about the president, but about his enemies to score political points.' It is impressive that our system ground slowly toward its conclusion. The idea that this was a stampede to get rid of the president is not right at all. This was a very measured process."

As a lawyer, Stern was impressed with the system. As a reporter, he admits he couldn't have asked for a more sensational story to cover.

"There were a lot of wonderful moments that were a journalist's dream in a sense," he said. "There was a lot of good copy."

• • • •

On September 5, 1975, the Mets sent their ace pitcher Tom Seaver—already with twenty wins—to the Shea Stadium mound against the St. Louis Cardinals. In the bottom of the third inning, with the game still scoreless and a runner on first, Mets leftfielder Mike Vail sent an Eric Rasmussen pitch over the fence to give the Mets a 2-0 lead. The Cardinals tied the score in the top of the fifth inning on back-o-back run-scoring hits by outfielders Bake McBride and Willie Davis.

The Mets regained the lead for good in the bottom of the sixth inning when first baseman Dave Kingman followed a Rusty Staub single with a two-run blast over the left-field fence. The Mets added an insurance run in the bottom of the seventh inning when Mike Vail singled home Del Unser. The 5-2 victory helped Seaver improve his record to 21-7. The Mets, as a team, moved to within five and a half games of first place with their seventy-third victory of the season. The game ended at 10:28 p.m. Eastern Daylight Time.

Less than ten hours earlier, President Ford was leaving a speaking engagement he had been attending in Sacramento, California. The president was walking from the building that hosted the speaking engagement, toward the California state capitol building, when a twenty-six-year-old woman drew a Colt .45 pistol from beneath the robe she was wearing and pointed it directly at Ford from point-blank range.

The gun never went off and a Secret Service agent grabbed the gun, forced it from the hand of the woman—Charles Manson follower Lynette "Squeaky" Fromme—and tackled her to the ground. She reportedly said, "It didn't go off. Can you believe it? It didn't go off."

President Ford refused to be rushed away by Secret Service agents, later stating that he was not scared—and really was quite apathetic—about the entire incident. He walked on to the California state house and resumed his day's schedule, meeting with California governor Jerry Brown. The two met for approximately a half hour, during which President Ford never mentioned the assassination attempt to Governor Brown. Once the two concluded their meeting, President Ford shared that an attempt had been made on his life.

In his presidential daily diary, the assassination attempt was entered as matter-of-factly as every other event the President attended that day. Under the time listed as 10:02 a.m. (Pacific Daylight Time), the diary notes: "The President walked from the Senator Hotel to the office of the Governor of California in the State Capitol. En route, the President was the target of an unsuccessful assassination attempt by alleged assassin Lynette Alice 'Squeaky' Fromme. Miss Fromme was toppled by Secret Service Agent Larry Buendorf."

Seventeen days later, the New York Yankees were at Shea Stadium to take on the first-place Boston Red Sox. Despite taking an early 2-0 lead on Thurman Munson's two-run blast in the bottom of the first inning, the Yankees gave up one run in the second inning and three more runs in the top of the sixth inning, as the Red Sox were on their way to a 6-4 victory, moving Boston to thirty games above .500 for the season. The loss dropped the Yankees to thirteen games behind the Red Sox in the standings.

Earlier that day, President Ford was in San Francisco, just outside the St. Francis Hotel, when Sarah Jane Moore, a mentally unstable accountant, tried to assassinate him. Her attempt was thwarted by a bystander, who instinctively grabbed her arm when she raised the gun toward the president from across the street. Although she fired one shot, it did not find its target. The bystander was a former Marine and Vietnam veteran named Oliver Sipple.

Moore had been known to the Secret Service, who evaluated the woman earlier in 1975. However, agents felt that Moore posed no danger to President Ford. Clearly, that evaluation was incorrect. After serving thirty-two years in prison, Moore said that she tried to assassinate Ford because she was "blinded by her radical political views." When interviewed about the event years later, Moore stated, "I am very glad I did not succeed. I know now that I was wrong to try."

Ford's political issues with New York City proved almost more dubious than the two attempts on his life.

As New York City plummeted into deeper and deeper financial ruin as 1975 arrived at its final months, President Ford was holding firm that he was not going to help. On October 29, he gave a speech denying federal assistance to prevent New York from total bankruptcy. That was what sparked the infamous—inaccurate—front-page headline in the New York Daily News: "Ford to City: Drop Dead: Vows He'll Veto Any Bail-Out." Ford never actually said those words, but the sentiment was the same and it was, after all, the Daily News.

Nevertheless, in 1975, Ford was trying to tell New York City to stand up on its own 16 million feet. In the end, the president eventually relented, signing the New York City Seasonal Financing Act of 1975, which extended $1.3 billion worth of federal loans to the city for three years.

"Only two months after saying or meaning or merely implying 'drop dead'—or, perhaps, resorting to tough love by holding the city's feet to the fire—Mr. Ford signed legislation to provide federal loans to the city, which were repaid with interest," Sam Roberts wrote in the *New York Times.*

It was in December of 1975—as the Jets and Giants closed out play at Shea Stadium—that Ford signed the bailout. Just weeks later, when looking back at his performance as the President of the United States in 1975, Ford defended his actions in regard to New York City.

"In the long haul, I think those decisions will be perceived as compassionate," Ford said. He added that the city would not have ever gotten to that point had the mayors over the past ten years "not been as generous handling the fiscal problems, wage settlements, pension programs, the city would be a lot better off today."

• • • •

The two assassination attempts of President Ford were just two of many terrorist attacks that took place around the world in 1975. Bombings were all the rage in the 1970s, first to make political statements and caused by antigovernment political groups. However, as the decade moved along, the attacks became more and more deadly.

Two of those deadly terrorist attacks that took place occurred in New York City, one in Manhattan and the other not far from Shea Stadium.

The first took place on January 24, when a bomb exploded at Fraunces Tavern in downtown Manhattan—on Pearl Street—killing four people and injuring dozens. The bomb exploded near the entrance of the building during lunchtime and damaged the tavern's annex. Most of the victims were dining upstairs. The Puerto Rican nationalist group F.A.L.N.—Fuerzas Armadas de Liberación Nacional Puertorriqueña (Armed Forces of Puerto Rican National Liberation)—took full responsibility for the blast. No one, however, was ever charged or prosecuted for the blast.

Eight days after the Jets lost the final football game of the 1975 regular season to the Dallas Cowboys, there was a devastating terrorist attack just two miles northwest of Shea Stadium. On December 29, a large bomb was detonated in a locker adjacent to a luggage carousel shared by Trans World Airlines and Delta Airlines at LaGuardia Airport.

The explosion blew out the floor and ceiling, started a fire in the terminal, killed eleven people, and injured nearly eighty others. At the time, the 1975 LaGuardia bombing was the most deadly attack on American soil since 1927, when forty-four people were killed at a school bombing in Michigan.

It was also the deadliest terrorist attack in New York City since a bomb went off in a parked horse-drawn wagon on Wall Street in 1920, killing more than three dozen people and injuring hundreds.

Like the bombing of Fraunces Tavern, the LaGuardia attack has never been solved and remains in many ways an act of terrorism that is lost in time. Several groups were suspected, including F.A.L.N., but no group took responsibility for the bombing.

One of the strongest leads in the case came a year later when a Croatian nationalist group hijacked an airplane and detonated a bomb in a locker. The Croatian hijackers never denied responsibility for the bombing at LaGuardia, but they also had no known motive.

"It remains unsolved and almost forgotten—except by those whose loved ones were killed or maimed," Terence G. McTigue, a former supervisor in the Police Department's bomb squad, told the *New York Times* in 2008.

• • • •

Archie Bunker—like all of the residents of Queens and the other boroughs of New York City—was under life's pressures as well. Still, by 1975, *All in the Family* was the top-rated show on television and already had inspired three direct or indirect spin-off situation comedies. The first was 1972's *Maude*—starring Edith Bunker's cousin—played by Bea Arthur. In 1974, the second spin-off was *Good Times*, which was actually a direct spin-off of *Maude*. It starred Esther Rolle as Florida Evans, who was the former maid on *Maude*. The most successful spinoff of *All in the Family* premiered in 1975 when *The Jeffersons* hit the airwaves. *The Jeffersons* starred Sherman Hemsley as George Jefferson, the cantankerous former neighbor of the Bunkers. In fact, *The Jeffersons* would end up lasting longer as a series than *All in the Family*.

In addition to *The Jeffersons*, there were many other shows launched successfully in 1975. *Wheel of Fortune*, *Barney Miller*, and the daytime soap *Ryan's Hope* all were born in 1975. However, perhaps no television show that began in 1975 had as much of an impact on popular culture as the show that would eventually be called *Saturday Night Live* did—which was filmed in, where else, New York City.

On Saturday night, October 11, the New York Giants were preparing to play their first-ever home game at Shea Stadium. For the past two seasons, the Giants had played their home campaign at the Yale Bowl in New Haven, Connecticut. It had been a disaster. For the 1973 and 1974 seasons combined, the Giants had won only one home game. Morale was very low. So when Wellington Mara decided to bring his team back to New York City for one last season—before his new complex in New Jersey was ready—team members and fans alike were excited.

The Giants were going to take on the Dallas Cowboys the next day. The Giants were off to a very slow start in 1975, losing two of the three games to open their season—all on the road. They were hoping that their "home" opener would be an elixir of sorts, as more than 56,000 fans were expected to be on hand to witness the Giants' opener in Queens.

That night, a new sketch-comedy variety show called *NBC's Saturday Night* (which would not change its name to *Saturday Night Live* for another two years) made its debut. Created by Lorne Michaels and developed by Dick Ebersol, *Saturday Night Live's* first cast included Laraine Newman, John Belushi, Jane Curtin, Gilda Radner, Dan Aykroyd, Garrett Morris, and Chevy Chase. Each week, a guest host would appear as well. On December 11, 1975, that guest host was stand-up comic George Carlin. It would be the first of only two times the comedy legend would host *SNL*—visiting again in 1984.

Before Carlin would take the stage for his opening monologue, *Saturday Night Live* opened with a sketch by soon-to-be-comedy-legend

John Belushi, as a European immigrant speaking with a professor, played by writer Michael O'Donoghue.

Carlin then officially ran through the audience to the stage and began his opening monologue, which could not have been more appropriate to start a comedy show in New York City in—of all years—1975. It was entitled "Baseball and Football," and could have easily been entitled "Shea Stadium."

After opening the monologue, Carlin got down to the nitty-gritty about both sports, particularly about the words used in discussing each of them. In one example, he distinguishes between the fact that you play football in a "stadium" and baseball in a "park." In another, he points out the difference between the words "penalty" and "error."

Chevy Chase ended the night's show by wishing everyone "a pleasant tomorrow."

Unfortunately, the New York Giants didn't appear to have been watching. Their tomorrow entailed yet another loss—dropping them to a start of 1-3. Their fans showed up, 56,511 strong, to cheer on Big Blue in Shea Stadium on a 58-degree day in Flushing. However, the Giants offense could not muster much of an attack against the Dallas defense, gaining just 173 total yards and a single touchdown. Although Giants quarterback Craig Morton actually had a better statistical day than Dallas' Roger Staubach, New York was unable to secure a victory. It had become a common theme of Giants home games. In games that were listed as "home" games on their schedule, none of which were actually at a Giants home, the team had won just one of their past thirteen games.

• • • •

In 1975, a family of four attending a Mets or Yankees game at Shea Stadium would need to spend a total of about thirty dollars for tickets, hot dogs, and sodas. If you took the subway to the game, it would cost you another 35 cents per person—laughable by today's standards. However, 1975 was a very different time. The price of a first-class postage stamp was just a dime; a gallon of gas cost 44 cents; and the price of a ticket to see a movie was about two dollars. Among the films released in 1975 were: *One Flew Over the Cuckoo's Nest*, *The Rocky Horror Picture Show*, *Monty Python and the Holy Grail*, *Dog Day Afternoon*, and *Tommy*.

However, no movie made as much of a forever impact on beachgoers as Steven Spielberg's *Jaws*. Starring Roy Scheider, Robert Shaw, and Richard Dreyfuss, *Jaws* was about a gigantic great white shark that menaces the small island community of Amity. The police chief played by Scheider, a marine scientist played by Dreyfuss, and a grizzled fisherman played by Shaw, set out to stop it.

The total budget for making *Jaws*, mechanical shark and all, was approximately eight million dollars. That cost was nearly paid for following the opening weekend in the United States alone. When the film premiered on more than four hundred screens June 22 and 23, it grossed more than seven million dollars. It became the first-ever summer blockbuster. In less than two months, it had become the highest grossing film of all time.

"If you think about *Jaws* for more than forty-five seconds you will recognize it as nonsense, but it's the sort of nonsense that can be a good deal of fun, if you like to have the wits scared out of you at irregular intervals," wrote Vincent Canby in the *New York Times*.

By the end of 1975, Jaws had grossed more than $190 million in the US. Overall, as of 2015, Jaws had grossed more than $470 million worldwide for theaters and rentals.

• • • •

While New York City continued its struggle, and the Mets, Yankees, Jets, and Giants were all having a Shea Stadium party, there were six other professional sports teams in New York that were also in action in 1975.

The most senior of those non-Shea Stadium teams was the New York Rangers of the National Hockey League. The Rangers, who had not won the Stanley Cup in thirty-five years, were extremely competitive during the early 1970s.

In 1971-72, the Rangers—led by three of the league's top scorers, Jean Ratelle, Vic Hadfield, and Rod Gilbert—reached the Stanley Cup Finals, only to fall to the Boston Bruins in six games. The following season, the Rangers returned to the playoffs, but lost in the semifinals to the Chicago Blackhawks. They lost in the semis again in 1973-74—this time in a grueling seven-game series against the Philadelphia Flyers.

The Rangers were among the elite teams in the National Hockey League and were ready to take that next step and possibly raise Lord Stanley's Cup. Enter the new kids on the block.

After paying the New York Rangers a nearly four million-dollar territorial fee, the New York Islanders entered the National Hockey League in time for the 1972-73 season. The Islanders played like the expansion team they were, losing sixty of their seventy-eight games in their opening season. The Islanders won twelve times and tied six games. They lost to the Rangers each of the six times the two teams faced off.

The following season, the Islanders were not much better, finishing the 1973-74 season with a record of 19-41-18. All of that added up to another last-place finish for the second-year team.

Things all changed in year three, however. The young Islanders—led by player such as Denis Povin, Clark Gillies, Bobby Nystrom, and Billy Harris—finished in third place in the new Patrick Division. The Islanders actually earned the same number of overall points as their rivals, the New York Rangers, but the Rangers had more victories, giving them second place. It didn't really matter—finishing second and third meant the Islanders were going to take on the Rangers in the first round of the 1975 playoffs.

Not many experts—or fans, for that matter—gave the Islanders much of a chance to take the series against the playoff-seasoned Rangers. It was, after all, the first time the Islanders were even appearing in a playoff series. However, they held their own and the two teams each won on home ice over the first two games of the series. The final, series-deciding game was played at Madison Square Garden on April 11, 1975.

Earlier that afternoon, Catfish Hunter and the New York Yankees lost their home opener at Shea Stadium against the Detroit Tigers. That evening, however, would change the hockey landscape in New York forever.

The Islanders looked like they were going to shock just about everyone after taking a 3-0 lead two periods in. However, the veteran Rangers squad fought back, scoring three times in the final period to tie the score and send the clinching game to sudden-death overtime. More than perhaps any other overtime, this one truly was sudden-death, or sudden-elation, depending on which side of the East River you were located. The Islanders' J. P. Parise scored eleven seconds into overtime to propel the Islanders past their rivals and into the second round of the playoffs. This was just the start of the excitement for the Islanders in 1975, though.

Beating the Rangers clearly took its toll on the Islanders, who quickly fell behind the Pittsburgh Penguins in the second round, three games to none. Only one team in the history of the National Hockey League, the 1942 Toronto Maple Leafs, had been able to erase such a deficit and advance in the playoffs.

Despite the Islanders' predicament, their coach—Al Arbour—remained not only cool and collected, but confident.

"He came into the locker room and said to us that 'if we don't believe we can win, stay on that side of the room,'" said Glenn "Chico" Resch, a rookie goaltender with the team. Resch had played about half of the regular-season games, but very few playoff games, leaving that to the more veteran goaltender, Billy Smith. "'Anyone who believes we can win, come over here on my side.' And of course we all went over with Al. Other coaches won, but as a complete package, nobody was better than Al. He was just so respectful of everyone. He always coached from a positive angle."

One of the biggest things Arbor was about to do before Game Four was insert his rookie goaltender.

"To inspire the club, [Islanders coach] Al Arbour makes a change in goal, inserting Glenn Resch, who has not seen action since the second game of the Ranger series," hockey historian Stan Fischler writes in his book. *The Triumphant Islanders: Hockey's New Dynasty.* "With the capacity crowd at Nassau Coliseum chanting 'Chico, Chico!' and with signs urging the Islanders to *Souvenez-vous les Maple Leafs* (Remember the Maple Leafs), the Islanders win, 3-1."

The Islanders still had a pulse, albeit a weak one.

"It was one thing to win Game Four, because it was like 'Okay, we won a game, great,'" Resch said. "But when we went into Pittsburgh and we beat them in Game Five—hockey more than any other sport—I think teams can sense a momentum change and we sensed that after Game Five."

The Islanders then went on to win Game Six at the Nassau Coliseum. Somehow, the Islanders and Penguins were now tied at three games apiece heading to Pittsburgh for a deciding Game Seven on April 26, 1975.

"Going into Game Seven, we knew that the first period was going to be critical," said Resch, who was playing in his fourth straight game. "I remember the game started and they just blitzed us. I got hit in the head right between the eyes with one shot right in that blue mask of mine, and they hit each goalpost within like a five-minute span. I remember thinking 'whoa.' But when they didn't score in the first, it reassured us that the unseen hand was still pulling the unseen rope in our direction. I think for them, they were just in disbelief thinking that this can't be happening."

The game remained scoreless into the third period, making it really feel like it was a sudden-death overtime game as the minutes and seconds ticked away in the third period. Finally, midway through the third period, captain Eddie Westfall scored to give the Islanders a 1-0 lead. However, soon after that goal, the Penguins' young gun, Pierre Larouche, broke in all alone on Resch, attempting to tie the score.

"I remember thinking that this guy is so tricky, I am going to try and surprise him with a poke check," Resch remembered. "They had a few more chances after that, but they were pretty much done when he didn't score. That was their one real chance."

The Islanders had accomplished the seemingly impossible—coming back from a three-games-to-none deficit to defeat the Pittsburgh Penguins.

"The locker room scene was pretty cool," Resch said. "You don't remember a lot of locker room scenes, but I remember I did a dance after we won and when someone asked me what dance it was, I said, 'Oh, that was the Chico Cha Cha.' It was exhilarating. After that, we always felt that we could win."

In the next round, the Islanders fell behind three games to none, once again. And once again, they fought back to force a deciding seventh game. This time, however, the Islanders' mojo had worn out, or was at least too tired. The Flyers took the series, winning the seventh game, 4-1. Still, the Islanders proved something very important to themselves in 1975. It validated their place in the league.

"It was the first time that I felt like a real NHLer," Resch said. "That I could really play with the best, and our team could play with the best."

While the Rangers and Islanders were fighting it out on the ice, the New York Knicks were having their own issues. The team was stunned following the 1973-74 season when superstar—and future Hall of Famer—Willis Reed announced his retirement. Injuries had worn down the big man, who was a seven-time all-star and had a career average of 18.7 points per game to go along with 12.9 rebounds per game.

After finishing with a record of 40-42, Red Holzman's team ended the 1974-75 season in third place of the Atlantic Division. They would face the Houston Rockets in the best-of-three opening round of the NBA Playoffs.

After splitting the first two games, the Knicks were blown out by the Rockets in Game Three by a score of 118-86, ending their very average season. Despite having future Hall of Famers Walt Frazier and Earl Monroe in the prime of their careers and future Hall of Famer Bill Bradley toward the end of his career, the Knicks could not make any winning moves in 1974-75. The forty victories was the team's lowest win total since the 1966-67 season. Just two years removed from winning the NBA championship—and one year removed from losing in the Eastern Conference Finals—the Knicks were one and done in the playoffs.

About 22 miles east of Madison Square Garden, at the Nassau Veterans Memorial Coliseum, a different brand of basketball was being played.

The New York Nets, playing in the rival American Basketball Association, had themselves a terrific regular season. Led by Julius Erving, the twenty-five-year-old phenom and the league's co-MVP, the Nets had a record of 58-26, good for second-best in the entire ABA. It also tied them with the Kentucky Colonels—who also had fifty-eight wins—for first place in the Eastern Division. Only the Denver Nuggets of the Western Division had more wins, with sixty-five.

One of the teams that finished behind the Nets in the Eastern Division was the Spirits of St. Louis, which had a record of 32-52 and finished twenty-six games behind New York in the standings. Even worse for St. Louis was the fact that the Nets had won all eleven games that the two teams had played during the 1974-75 season by an average of more than seventeen points. It was going to be a layup of sorts for Erving and the defending ABA-champion Nets.

Erving was confident in his team heading into the playoffs, mostly because he had had great support from teammates, such as Billy Paultz and Larry Kenon.

"My main goal is to be a complete player," Erving said after a work-out at Nassau Coliseum before the playoffs began. "I think this year my teammates have made things easier for me. I know that night after night I don't have to go out and do everything."

The Nets took the opener of the series, handing the Spirits of St. Louis its twelfth-straight defeat at the hands of New York. Then, everything changed. The Spirits of St. Louis somehow found new life and the Nets somehow couldn't match their intensity. Then, the unthinkable happened—the Spirits of St. Louis came into the Nets' home and attempted to put the final nails into New York's coffin.

Late in the fourth quarter, the Nets—who had led by as many as sixteen points in the game—looked for sure as if they would force a Game Six back in St. Louis.

However, with twenty seconds left and leading by a single point, the Nets botched an inbound play, as Erving—under pressure from St. Louis's Don Adams—dribbled the ball off of his leg and into the back court. The violation gave possession to the Spirits of St. Louis. Down by one point, the Spirits inbounded the ball to Freddie Lewis, who dribbled to the top of the key and, with only three seconds remaining, hit a jumper to win the game—and, more importantly—the series. It was a stunning end to the Nets season. The lead of the *New York Times* game story told readers everything they needed to know: "Improbably, but irresistibly, the Spirits of St. Louis completed their upset of the American Basketball Association champions."

Following the clincher, a disheartened Erving—who led all scorers with 34 points—appeared to be in disbelief.

"In our hearts," he said, "we feel we have the better team. But we didn't play better basketball."

Erving's teammate Bill Melchionni—who had 11 points and 11 assists in the game—summed things up best following the game.

"We didn't respond to the challenge," he said. "That's what is so disheartening. We played like a team happy to be in the playoffs instead of like the defending champions."

This soon became the playoff series that is often forgotten by New York fans, since the Spirits of St. Louis—and the ABA itself—are no longer around to remember. When the ABA merged into the NBA, the Spirits did not make the journey and folded.

In 1975, New York City had two other non-Shea Stadium teams for fans to root for—the New York Cosmos and the New York Sets.

The Cosmos were considered the strongest team of the North American Soccer League, the premiere soccer league in the United States during its lifespan of 1970 through 1985.

Following the 1974 season, when the Cosmos finished toward the bottom of their division, they acquired by far the greatest and most famous soccer player of all time in June of 1975—Brazilian superstar Pelé. The Cosmos agreed to pay Pelé an outrageous salary of $1.4 million per season. Nevertheless, such a steep salary seemed to pay off for the team almost immediately. His first game at the Cosmos' home field—Downing Stadium on Randall's Island—was against the Dallas Tornado. It was televised to twenty-two countries and covered by more than three hundred press members.

Downing Stadium, which had been open since 1936, had hosted many important sporting events, such as men's and women's Olympic trials, Negro League baseball games, football games, and international soccer matches. The first event ever at Downing Stadium—originally known as Randall's Island Stadium—was the 1936 Men's Olympic Trials, during which Jesse Owens showed off his greatness.

The stadium was also the home of many concerts throughout the years, including performers such as the Duke Ellington Orchestra, Jimi Hendrix, Grand Funk Railroad, and Pearl Jam.

For Pelé's first game against Dallas, the old pitch—short on grass—was spray-painted green to make it look like a more appealing venue for the television broadcasts.

Pelé alone was not enough to propel the Cosmos into the playoffs, though, and the following season, the team acquired stars such as Giorgio Chinaglia. The Cosmos subsequently moved to play its home games at Yankee Stadium and then at Giants Stadium—winning multiple championships in the late 1970s.

The Sets, meanwhile, are definitely the least-remembered team in New York from 1975. In their second year of existence in the World Team Tennis League, the Sets' roster included Billie Jean King (who had been traded to the Sets before the season), Stan Smith, and Ilie Nastase. The Sets were in the Eastern Division, along with the Pittsburgh Triangles, the Boston Lobsters, the Indiana Loves, and the Cleveland Nets. The Western Conference consisted of teams, such as the San Francisco Golden Gaters, Phoenix Racquets, Los Angeles Strings, Hawaii Leis, and San Diego Friars.

The Sets finished second in 1975 and advanced to the Eastern Division Playoffs, where they lost to the Lobsters. Prior to 1975, the Lobsters had been the Philadelphia Freedoms—led by player-coach King—but were purchased before the season and moved north.

After King—the first woman to serve as a coach for a professional sports team that included male players—signed on to play for the Freedoms, her good friend Elton John wrote a song for her to wish her luck in the league's inaugural year. The song actually came out in February of 1975, after the Freedoms played their last game in Philadelphia before moving to Boston, and King had been traded to New York. In any event, the song long outlasted the Lobsters, the Sets, and the entire World Team Tennis League. "Philadelphia Freedom" went to Number One in the charts and was arguably the best thing to ever come out of the short-lived league, which folded in 1978.

• • • •

On April 18, 1975, nearly ten years after the Beatles first stepped onto the infield stage at Shea Stadium—and five years after the band's breakup became official—John Lennon did an interview in New York for BBC2 program, *The Old Grey Whistle Test*. Lennon, of course, was asked the question he had been asked probably every day since the Beatles broke up. This time, the question was posed a little differently by interviewer Bob Harris, who not only asked if the Beatles would get back together, but also asked "much more importantly—would that reunion be a good idea?"

"That's another point altogether whether it would be a good idea or not," said a relaxed John Lennon, wearing a cap and his trademark round eyeglasses. "You see it's strange because at one period when they asked me that, I'd say 'Nah, never, what the hell, go back? Not me.' And then there came a period where I started to think, 'Yeah, why not, maybe we'll make a record.' Everybody always envisions the stage show. To me, if we work together in the studio . . . the stage show is something else . . . if we have something to say in the studio, okay. It's never gotten to a position where each one of us have wanted to do it at the same time."

To the second part of the question, on whether it would be worth it, Lennon answered somewhat more philosophically.

"That is answered by if we want to do it," Lennon said. "If we wanted to do it, then it would be worth it. If we got into the studio and we turned each other on again, then it would be worth it. The music is the music. If we make something that we think is worthwhile, than it goes out. But it's pie in the sky. I don't care either way, if someone wants to pull it together, I'll go along. I'm not in the mood to pull it together, that's for sure."

Unfortunately, it never got pulled together. Later that night, Lennon performed live at New York City's Waldorf Astoria Hotel during a gala all-star special, organized for television broadcast, called "A Salute to Sir Lew Grade: The Master Showman." Lennon sang three songs, closing with a revamped take on his hit "Imagine."

Neither the Mets, nor the Yankees played at Shea Stadium that night—the night that marked the final time that John Lennon would ever perform live in public.

• • • •

By 1975, the nation was trying to get past the Richard Nixon saga. Nixon had resigned from office on August 8, 1974, flying away in his helicopter—leaving the nation in the hands of Gerald Ford. However, Nixon was summoned back to Washington in May of 1975. Already pardoned by Ford, Nixon had full immunity for anything that he would say to the Watergate Special Prosecution Force, which called upon him to answer questions. Health issues, however, prevented Nixon from traveling to the nation's capital, so he traveled from his home to nearby San Mateo, California, to answer questions.

Nixon was questioned over two days—June 23 to June 24, 1975—in order to get answers as part of various investigations being conducted by the January 7, 1974, Grand Jury for the District of Columbia (the third Watergate Grand Jury). Nixon was questioned on many issues, including the 18-and-a-half-minute gap in the White House tape recording of Nixon and H. R. Haldeman from 1972.

According to the official transcripts, Nixon was asked—in several different ways—if he remembered the substance of the conversation he had with Haldeman. Nixon repeatedly replied that he did not. He was asked a similarly directed question and responded that he had been asked that question already.

"I don't mean to argue with counsel, because having sometimes been on the other side of the table as a congressman, you do sometimes come back to the same question without intending to be repetitive, but I am pointing out I have never heard this conversation that you have alluded to, this so called eighteen and a half minute gap, and I add in that period I did not listen to the conversation you have alluded to, this tape. This tape was not in my possession. I didn't have possession of it. It didn't come into my possession before and I have never had it in my possession," said Nixon, according to the official Grand Jury transcript.

"The point is that—let me say, when I talk about a tape being in my possession, I have noted from the records here that various people have indicated that among those who had access to the tapes was the president at all times. What I am saying is to the best of my recollection—I didn't even recall where they were kept—to the best of my recollection, unless they were obtained by somebody else and brought to me for the purpose of listening. I have no recollection of ever having heard this particular tape you refer to. And in checking the record, I find that, or I should say my counsel, I guess, checked the records—I hope they have—I find no indication that this tape was ever checked out to me."

On the same day that Nixon was making these statements, the St. Louis Cardinals swept the Mets in a doubleheader played at Shea Stadium. The Mets did not score a single run.

CHAPTER 6

When Baseball Ended, and the Football Season Began

On August 25, 1975, singer-songwriter Bruce Springsteen released his third studio album entitled, *Born to Run*. It was a critical and commercial success and thrust Springsteen into the mainstream of rock and roll. He appeared on the covers of both *Time* and *Newsweek* magazines—in fact, the personification of mainstream. Despite having two earlier albums, by 1975 Springsteen had arrived.

New York Jets running back John Riggins also appeared to be born to run in 1975 and the Jets could not have been happier. Like Springsteen, Riggins had experienced some success in the early 1970s, but it wasn't until 1975 that Riggins too had truly arrived, and—as it would turn out—depart.

"John was a fine ballplayer and he's a deserving Hall of Famer," said former Jets' tight end Richard Caster, who was a teammate of Riggins. "He was a track champion that paid off when he came out of the backfield. You didn't want to be in his way."

Despite Riggins's success running the football in 1975, the Jets struggled mightily. Perhaps it was that fact, as well as the millions of dollars he was handed, that had Riggins rushing to the Washington

Redskins following his thousand-plus-yard Pro Bowl season with New York.

• • • •

When baseball officially came to an end on September 28, it left behind a battered and bruised playing field for the Jets and Giants. Shea Stadium's head groundskeeper, Pete Flynn, and his staff had done their best, but once the football season got under way, it was virtually impossible to keep the field in anything resembling good condition.

"It was nonstop," Flynn said. "There was no grass left by the end of it. We couldn't get a grip on it at all."

But it was not only the field that posed problems for players at Shea Stadium.

"Without question, Shea was the most challenging place to kick a football," the late Giants punter Dave Jennings had been quoted as saying about his time playing in Queens. "The wind was always in your face no matter which way you turned. The people, the fans, the grounds crew were great, but I was so happy that we only played there for one year because of the conditions."

Jennings was not overstating the chaos that the winds at Shea caused. In December of 1975, the National Weather Service concluded a ten-year study at nearby LaGuardia Airport, which predicted that the final month of football season would have the Jets and Giants enduring winds of twenty-five miles per hour. But it's not just the speed of the winds. Because of the shape of Shea Stadium, with its huge open end, the winds created updrafts, downdrafts, and cyclonic-like swirls.

"People don't think I'm crazy anymore," Jets punter Greg Gantt told the *New York Times* midway through the 1975 season. "When the Jets played at Shea, people thought I was making excuses. But now the Giants can tell you about the winds, too."

Giants' quarterback Craig Morton agreed with the kickers when speaking to reporters in 1975.

"There's no way you can throw the ball in that wind to certain parts of the field," Morton said. "I always used to wonder why Joe Namath's completion average was down around forty-eight percent. But now I know."

• • • •

The New York Jets were never quite comfortable in Shea Stadium, despite the fact that—like the Mets—the Jets had called Shea home since 1964. By the time 1975 rolled around, the Jets found themselves having to wait not just for the Mets to finish their season before kicking off their campaign, but they had to also wait for the Yankees to finish their campaign.

Things officially became a scheduling nightmare, when the New York Giants joined the party at Shea Stadium. If either the Mets or the Yankees would have reached the postseason in 1975—not to mention the World Series—football would have been relegated to cram fourteen games into just nine weeks. Baseball, as it always had, took precedence at Shea. Fortunately for the Jets and Giants—and the NFL—the Yankees and Mets cooperated by having subpar seasons.

Before the Jets could even get started in 1975, however, they ran into a roadblock of a different sort when the New England Patriots refused to play the final exhibition game. The Patriots' players were taking a hard line because of the fact that the NFL owners had not signed a new labor agreement with the players' union. However, the Patriots were hardly on solid ground. Only the Jets, Giants, Washington Redskins, and Detroit Lions recognized the Patriots' strike. And even then, players were divided.

The Jets' players voted to support the strike—despite the strong opposition of star quarterback Joe Namath—and the team walked out of camp the week of their season opener at Buffalo. The Patriots' strike had little real strength, however, and was considered more of a farce than a serious negotiation tactic. Five days after New England players walked out of camp and just before the season opener, the Patriots returned. With no strike left to support, the Jets too returned to work.

The Jets—who actually had to play their first four games on the road in 1974—ended up playing their first two games in 1975 on the road, opening up in Buffalo against the division-rival Bills. It was an opener the Jets would rather forget. The Bills—led by running back O. J. Simpson's 173 rushing years and two touchdowns—rolled over the Jets, 42-14.

One of the few bright spots in the opener for the Jets was the performance by tight end Richard Caster, who caught six passes for 103 yards and one touchdown. Caster, who was coming off of a terrific season in 1974—being named to the Pro Bowl for the second time in three years—seemed to be prepared for a great season.

After that first loss, the Jets regrouped for their trip to Kansas City against the Chiefs. After an average first game of the season, Riggins rushed for 145 yards and two touchdowns to lead the Jets to a 30-24 victory. The Jets managed to split their first two road games of the season and returned to Shea Stadium for their season opener with high hopes.

On a relatively warm early October Sunday afternoon, 57,365 fans packed into Shea to launch the 1975 Shea football campaign. They would not be disappointed.

The Jets, led by quarterback Joe Namath's four touchdown passes, blew past the New England Patriots, 36-7. Despite Riggins's huge individual performance one week earlier, the Jets ran the ball by committee against New England, with three different backs—Riggins, Steve Davis, and Carl Garrett—each getting at least eleven carries. That group rushing attack, combined with quarterback Joe Namath completing fifteen of twenty-one passes to six different receivers, propelled New York and sent the fans home happy.

Two of those happy fans arrived a little late for the contest, but were still thrilled by what they had witnessed. With the Jets comfortably ahead 22-0 midway through the third quarter, Hirohito—the Emperor of Japan—and his wife made their way into a bulletproof royal box, which was purchased for the occasion. Hirohito had been invited to attend an NFL game by President Ford one year earlier, and the timing of the Jets-Patriots matchup worked well with the emperor's visit to New York City. Arrangements were made months before the season began and security was established by Japanese and American secret service.

Still, even with all of the security, there was an unforeseen issue, as the caravan carrying the royal couple arrived in front of Shea Stadium's main entrance. After Emperor Hirohito emerged from the car, his wife's high hairdo got stuck on the top of the door frame of the limousine as she tried to exit.

"Three or four Japanese secret servicemen got her untangled," Jets business manager John Free said.

During the ensuing thirteen minutes of the game, Japan's royalty witnessed Namath throwing two touchdown passes—both to Jerome Barkum.

"They probably looked easy to him," Namath joked after the game. "Just throw it up in the air."

Hirohito was on a very tight schedule during his tour of the United States, which is why he and his wife did not arrive until the second half of the game, following lunch with the Rockefellers. The royal couple was supposed to leave Shea soon after arriving and watching a bit of the game, but Hirohito reportedly refused to leave until the Jets scored again.

"He was supposed to leave," Jets President Phil Iselin said after the game, "but we were on the six-yard line and he wanted to see another touchdown."

When Namath hit Barkum on a quick, four-yard touchdown pass, Hirohito got his wish and was able to leave Shea Stadium a happy man.

"He was very enthusiastic about everything he saw," NFL Commissioner Pete Rozelle said following the Jets' victory, sharing even more details than the public probably was interested in. "He had a bad cold and he was coughing a lot, but he really seemed to be enjoying himself."

Still, when asked about meeting the players, Hirohito let his love of baseball—which was already very popular in Japan—shine through.

"I'd like to get Catfish Hunter's autograph," the Emperor responded.

The Jets played that day at Shea like they couldn't be beaten. The reality was just the opposite. New York would not win another game at home all season.

"[Shea Stadium] was not a cool place to be after a while because the fans got real angry and impatient," Caster said. "If I had a miscue or dropped a pass, they let you know that they were not happy. It was not fun."

It also was not an overly fun experience for the Jets to be sharing their stadium with the Giants in 1975. Plus, the field conditions—which had been bad for baseball—had deteriorated to terrible for football.

"We certainly would have preferred to have a stadium to ourselves," Caster said. "We didn't have any ill feelings toward the Giants and it really just was what it was. We did the best we could. I remember running into guys like Spider Lockhart and Bob Tucker. We had other things to talk about really, other than a quick chuckle about the idea of the condition of the field. How it was precarious while we were trying to run in certain areas of the field."

"Precarious" was an extremely positive word to use when describing the playing conditions during the 1975 football season at Shea Stadium.

"The field was never really a solid foundation," Caster said. "I remember against the Miami Dolphins, there was a comment made by one of the announcers that [Joe] Namath was 'doing a little gardening' before the play. That was really Joe kicking some dirt down and stomping it back into place like you would do on a golf course when you replace your divot. Then he got back under center, dropped back, and cracked one to me right down the middle. You were always conscious of the fact that you had to know what was prone to happen if you didn't come into a cut with some real body control. If you really just let it go like you were on a normal field, you could find yourself on the turf itself."

That game against the Dolphins was one of the most embarrassing moments of the 1975 season for the Jets. Namath was off target for the entire contest, completing just eight passes to Jets receivers, and six passes to Miami defenders. At the end of the day, the Jets had lost at home, 43-0, in front of only 47,191 at Shea Stadium—more than ten thousand fewer fans than had attended the opener.

One week later, the Jets hosted the Baltimore Colts for what would end up being one of the highest-scoring games of the year. In the end, the Colts would come out on top, 45-28. Namath rebounded to complete nineteen of twenty-eight passes, and threw for three touchdowns. Perhaps his most exciting completion of the game did not result in a touchdown—or did it?

Backed up on the Jets' own ten-yard line, Namath whipped a pass to Caster over the middle.

"The field was pretty solid down by the open end of the stadium," Caster remembered. "[Baltimore] went into a run coverage, what they called double-double, and it left the middle of the field open. We always had a standing audible that Joe and I could actually just look at one another and he would make a gesture and I knew to break my route into that open area. He would pop it right in there."

Once he had the ball in his hands, the speedy Caster took off, streaking toward the closed area of Shea Stadium. Caster nearly outran everyone, only to be caught inside the one-yard line.

"I always make an excuse for myself getting caught on the one-yard-line, because I was just coming back from a recent hamstring pull," Caster said. "I was still able to catch it though and outrun everyone before I finally got caught. I actually really thought I had gotten into the end zone, but the officials said no. That was a play that started on a very fast track and as I got farther down the field, I hit the slower part of the field that I always felt affected the outcome of that play."

Had there been instant replay in 1975, Caster feels he would have been awarded a touchdown.

"I would hope so, I still think I laid the ball out enough where it did break the plane," Caster said. "Yes, I do think it could have been ruled a touchdown, along with some others I had during my career. That's one of those plays that you can look back on from your career that become indelible, no matter how much time goes by."

Tight end Richard Caster, left, had an all-pro season as Joe Namath's go-to receiver in 1975. *Courtesy of thegoldenageofphotography.com*

Caster would have plenty of big plays in 1975 and once again become one of Namath's favorite receivers.

"That was something that any of us as receivers wanted to happen, that we became a prime target for Joe," Caster said. "We had so many years where we had Joe on the team when he was injured and wasn't able to play. It was very disappointing and disheartening. I played with Joe for five or six years, and the only years that I made the Pro Bowl is when Joe was healthy. He certainly made a difference in our ability to be successful as an offense. We loved to play with Joe. We knew we had our best chance to win when Joe Namath was under center."

While Namath started thirteen of the Jets' fourteen games in 1975, he was hardly productive, throwing twenty-eight interceptions compared to fifteen touchdowns. Injuries—and a desire to throw the ball up for grabs—had taken a toll on Namath, who led the National Football League in interceptions in both 1974 and 1975. The fact of the matter was, Namath had thrown more interceptions than touchdowns every season since 1969 and victories were getting harder and harder to come by.

In April of 1975, in fact, it appeared as though Namath would not even be under center for the Jets—and not because of an injury. Namath was being wooed by the fledgling World Football League, which had been luring many other established NFL players to defect. Players such as L. C. Greenwood, Gerry Philbin, and Larry Csonka had decided to take the money and—literally—run. Namath was offered a $4 million contract to play for the Chicago Winds franchise. The offer included a $500,000 bonus, a $500,000 guaranteed salary for three years, and $100,000 per year for the next twenty years. Plus, Namath would receive a 50 percent ownership in the New York franchise, which was expected to debut in 1976. Namath would also be allowed to leave Chicago and play for that New York franchise.

Namath seriously considered Chicago's offer and, according to various newspaper reports, was leaning toward joining the Winds, who had spent much of their time and money trying to lure Namath.

However, in the end, Namath decided to re-sign with the Jets. The Chicago Winds were crushed and folded five weeks into the 1975 season. Namath's rejection of the WFL also caused it to lose its national television contract. The network that was carrying the league—the TVS Television Network—specifically had told league organizers that only having Namath in the league would lead to the national deal. When that didn't happen, the WFL became an invisible league.

Following the 1975 season, the WFL ceased operations.

Namath and the Jets, meanwhile, were finding victories extremely hard to come by. After defeating the Patriots at Shea Stadium, the Jets went on to lose eight straight games, five of which came at home. During the slide, New York was outscored 277-111.

Six games into the losing streak, and three days after a 52-19 loss in Baltimore to the Colts, Charley Winner was fired as the Jets' head coach. Offensive coordinator Ken Shipp was named interim head coach and would lead the Jets through the remaining five weeks of the season.

Winner had a rough tenure as head coach of the Jets. He was hired prior to the 1974 season and needed a six-game winning streak to close out the year to finish with a mark of 7-7. His 2-7 start in 1975 was too much for him to overcome, or the Jets to stand by and watch.

The Jets finally won their third game of the season in Week Twelve, when they traveled to New England and defeated the Patriots for the second time of the season. Led by Riggins's two touchdowns, the Jets went on to a 30-28 victory—the only win of Ken Shipp's head coaching career.

After the first thirteen games of the season, Riggins was knocking on the door of Jets' history. No Jet had ever cracked the one-thousand mark for rushing yards. On a 27-degree day—15 degrees with the wind chill—Shea Stadium's playing field was more like a frozen dirt patch than a football field. Still, Riggins gained the yardage he needed against the Dallas Cowboys, finishing the season with 1,005 total rushing yards.

That was the only bright spot for the Jets that day, however, as the Cowboys won the game 31-21. The Jets' season had mercifully come to an end—with three wins and eleven losses.

• • • •

The Jets did not see a major difference in their 1975 attendance figures compared to the 1974 campaign. Overall, the Jets averaged about two thousand fewer fans per game in 1975. The Jets did, however, outdraw the Giants during the season, but only by a few hundred fans. Still, the Giants were fine with the overall numbers.

During the 1974 season at the Yale Bowl, the Giants had averaged 45,686 fans per game in a stadium that held more than sixty-four thousand fans. However, that was a bit misleading on the high side. If you took out the game against the Jets that season, which was a sellout, the Giants' per game average fell to just over forty-two thousand fans per game.

So when the Giants' attendance numbers for Shea Stadium at the end of the season averaged more than fifty-one thousand fans per game, the Giants were thrilled. The Giants were attracting many of their old fans back, as well as some new die-hard fans that normally would not have had the opportunity to attend a game.

"I was thrilled because I lived in Queens and for me to get to the Bronx to see a Giants game was very difficult," said television executive Sol Steinberg, who remembers how excited he was as a sixteen-year-old Giants fan when the team announced it was ending its short-lived tenure in Connecticut. "It was the Q28 bus to Flushing and then I took the 7 train right to Shea Stadium. I remember going to the game it felt very strange. It wasn't our home and we didn't belong there. I remember looking at the Giants down on the field and even though they were wearing their home blue uniforms, but something about it just didn't feel right."

• • • •

Giants fans were outraged when the team announced in 1971 that it would be moving to New Jersey. However, the simple fact was, the

Giants were going to get a state-of-the-art football-only facility that would benefit both the team and the fans.

In 1972, however, building a sports complex in the Hackensack Meadowlands was fraught with obstacles. There were many environmental concerns, and wildlife protections needed to be guaranteed.

The original plan called for the 750-acre facility to include the football stadium, a baseball stadium, a thoroughbred and harness-racing track, a hockey and basketball arena, a hotel, park, zoo, and aquarium.

"Ecologists say it will be an environmental disaster and will destroy the essential character of the Meadows, the tidal marshes that give sanctuary to the region's wildlife," writer Fred Ferretti said in the *New York Times*. "Other groups, including residents from among the fourteen communities surrounding the Meadowlands area, are challenging the constitutionality of the New Jersey Sports and Exposition Authority, which will build and operate the complex."

Still, New Jersey's Department of Environmental Protection and the Hackensack Meadowlands Development Commission both approved the construction, which was to begin in late November of 1972.

By the end of March 1973, the clearing of the land had been under way for about a month. In essence at that time it was just piles of dirt occupied by thousands of muskrats—and rats. Yes, muskrats—and rats.

"If you think the place looks like a mess now, you should have seen it a month ago," Sonny Werblin, once the president of the Jets and now chairman of the New Jersey Sports and Exposition Authority, told reporters.

The biggest part of the early days of construction was the erection of coffer dams around the perimeter of the stadium site. Water rose very high in the Meadowlands—as high as eight feet above ground level. Since the playing surface of the football field was planned to be four feet below sea level, drainage lagoons needed to be created and dams needed to be built.

"The muskrats will migrate someplace else," said Joe Ostroski, the project's co-manager, to reporters, "but the rats will have to be killed so they don't wind up on other people's property."

In December of 1974, the Giants signed the final contract to play in the New Jersey Meadowlands. The stadium was expected to be ready for the start of the 1976 football season.

• • • •

By far the strangest football weekend of the 1975 season came on November 15 and 16, when Sunday's game between the Giants and Philadelphia Eagles was preceded by a Saturday matchup between legendary coach Eddie Robinson's Grambling State University and Norfolk State of Virginia in the Whitney M. Young Memorial Football Classic. It was the fifth straight year that Grambling had participated in the charity game, which had been held in past years at Yankee Stadium.

The game was billed in southern newspapers as a battle of champions, with national Black College champions Grambling State facing Norfolk State, champions of the Central Intercollegiate Athletic Association.

Sponsored jointly by the New York Urban League and the Coca-Cola Bottling Company of New York, the Classic drew more than 215,000 fans for its first four games.

Since its inception, proceeds from the game have helped to leverage over $20 million in Whitney M. Young Jr. Educational Scholarships awarded to nearly four thousand college bound students. Whitney M. Young Jr., after whom the scholarship was named, was president of the National Urban League.

The trip to Shea was definitely a road trip to remember for Grambling's sophomore quarterback Doug Williams.

"Going to play at Shea Stadium—for me—all I was thinking was that Joe Namath played here," said Williams, who thirteen years later as a member of the Washington Redskins would go on to be named the Most Valuable Player of Super Bowl XXII. "Coach Robinson always used to tell us that anything that was worth a damn eventually had to go through, or come from, New York."

For Williams the trip to Shea was a personal one, because he was able to play on the same field where Tommie Agee—who attended Grambling—celebrated a world championship with the Mets in 1969.

"My brother had played baseball with Tommie Agee at Grambling," Williams said. "So for me that was big. But just being able to play in New York, and to play at Shea Stadium, was a blessing for us."

Grambling won the game, their fifth straight win in the Classic.

• • • •

In 1975, John Mara—the oldest son of the Giants' co-owner—was a senior at Boston College. His father, meanwhile, had been taking nonstop abuse since announcing that New York's historic football team would be leaving New York City and heading to New Jersey.

While waiting for their new home to be built, the Giants played the 1973 and 1974 seasons at the Yale Bowl in New Haven, Connecticut. This only further frustrated Giants players and fans. So prior to the 1975 season, Wellington Mara agreed to moved his team back to New York City—for one season—and play at Shea Stadium.

"I would take the shuttle down from Boston to LaGuardia and then go over to Shea and it was just a miserable period for us," John Mara said. "I remember a sign being hung from the upper deck at Shea Stadium which said 'Impeach Mara.' It was not a good time for us. I don't remember the specific games, but I remember leaving unhappy on many different occasions heading back to LaGuardia to go back to school."

The previous two seasons had been miserable for the Giants, who won just one home game at the Yale Bowl. Things did not improve all that much at Shea Stadium for the Giants.

Bill Arnsparger—who had been a defensive guru for the Miami Dolphins in the early 1970s—was in his second year as the Giants head coach. Arnsparger proved to be less of a guru as a head coach in New York.

"Bill was in his second year as a head coach and we thought he was going to be a great head coach," John Mara said. "He had been the architect of the no-name defense with the Dolphins and he was a so-called genius defensive coordinator. That was the first time in my life that I came to the realization that just because you are a great coordinator, it does not necessarily mean you can make the next step to head coach."

Still, Mara acknowledges that while Arnsparger was not a good fit as the Giants' head coach, it was not entirely his fault. Arnsparger had gone from ruling Miami's no-name defense to heading New York's no-name roster.

"In fairness to him, our organization was not set up sufficiently to provide him with the proper talent," Mara said, referring to the poor personnel decisions the franchise was making. None was arguably worse than acquiring quarterback Craig Morton from the Dallas Cowboys in 1974 in exchange for the Giants' first-round draft pick in 1975. The fact was that the Giants needed a quarterback, which caused them to sacrifice their future in more ways than one.

"We were so desperate to get a quarterback and Dallas went on to select Randy White, who went on to terrorize us for like the next fourteen years," Mara said. "We were just in a bad period organization-wise back then and it just added to the misery of us being nomads going from Yankee Stadium to the Yale Bowl to Shea Stadium to waiting to see if Giants Stadium was ever going to be finished."

White went on to a Hall of Fame career for the Cowboys, playing in nine Pro Bowls, three NFC Championship Games, and one Super Bowl. He was named to the NFL's All-Decade Team of the 1980s.

The Giants' end of the trade did not fare that well. Craig Morton was playing in 1975 with what was, for the most part, a translucent offensive line. Prior to the start of the season, it was unclear if Morton would be wearing the Giants' blue at all.

Like Joe Namath, Morton too was lured by the big cash promises of the World Football League. Unlike Namath, however, Morton signed a deal with the Houston Texans of the WFL while he was still a member of the Dallas Cowboys in 1974. Morton was a backup to quarterback Roger Staubach and asked repeatedly to be traded. Dallas had refused his requests.

"I had to take the initiative on my own," Morton said at that time. "At the time, the Cowboys weren't going to trade me and I was either going to move or not play at all."

Then, Dallas traded Morton to the Giants and Morton suddenly had no interest in playing in the WFL. Morton apparently had a clause in his WFL contract that stated if the Houston Texans ceased operations, he would be a free agent. When the Texans re-located to Louisiana following the 1974 season, Morton believed that the clause applied.

"I feel I upheld my end of the WFL contract," Morton said after meeting with Giants officials in April of 1975. "If the Houston Texans were playing, I'd be playing for them. But they're not playing."

The Giants' brass agreed, backing the man they wanted to have return as their starting quarterback. Although the fact was, Morton's contract with the Cowboys, which was inherited by the Giants after the trade, expired on May the first.

"According to our attorney's interpretation," Andy Robustelli, the Giants' Director of Operations, told reporters, "we see a break in the law. But the NFL will have to decide that before we can act."

Morton was clear that he wanted to return to the Giants.

"I'm where I want to be," the quarterback said. "I'm not trying to throw anything in the faces of the WFL, but I feel that I am a free agent."

As it turns out, Morton would never play a game in the WFL. There may have been times, however, that he wished he had.

After starting the season with a 4-3 record, the Giants plunged into a downward spiral. The Giants lost five straight games, with the final loss of that streak being a painful 21-0 defeat at the hands of the Baltimore Colts at Shea Stadium. In the loss, Morton was sacked seven times.

"Sure, it makes me upset," Morton said following the game, "but there's not much you can do but just keep going out and play. There

ENTER GATE B
FIELD BOX TIER
SEC. BOX / ROW SEAT
64D 4
$8.00 (7.41 + TAX .59)
ACCT. NO. 265350
GAME 7
GIANTS
AT
SHEA STADIUM
VS
NEW ORLEANS
SAINTS
GAME 7
SUN., DEC. 14, 1975, 1:00 P.M.
$8.00 (7.41 + TAX .59)
FIELD BOX TIER
64D 4
SEC. BOX / ROW SEAT

isn't any reason to say anything to [my offensive line]. If they're playing bad, it's not me that's going to change the way they play."

Through the first twelve weeks of the season, the Giants offense averaged just 13.5 points per game and allowed forty-four sacks for losses, totaling more than three hundred yards.

In 1975, the Giants would manage to win only five games—and only two of those victories came at Shea Stadium. It was another dark season for the once-proud NFL franchise.

"The hardest thing was seeing how much pain it caused my father because he wanted so desperately to bring our team back to where it had been in the 1950s and early 1960s," said John Mara. "He kept trying all of these desperate moves to get us back there and we ended up trading a lot of our draft picks and tried to put a quick fix on it and that was just not the way to go. It's a period of time that still haunts us."

Still, while he views the one season at Shea Stadium as more of an oddity than anything else, John Mara is careful to never forget that one year in Flushing.

"It serves as motivation for me to never want to slip back into that hole that we were in," Mara said. "I learned a lot by going through it, but it's not something I want to have to repeat."

CHAPTER 7

The Aftermath of 1975

FOLLOWING THE COMPLETION OF THE 1975 football season, the Giants packed their bags and checked out of the Shea Motel. The Yankees had already done as much, making the ten-mile journey back to the Bronx and their new, $160 million version of Yankee Stadium. The Giants had a bit of a longer drive, hopping over the George Washington Bridge and heading into neighboring New Jersey and their long-awaited new stadium.

When the Yankees returned to the Bronx for the 1976 season, according to Marty Appel, "it seemed like we were never away, it was great."

Much had changed since the Yankees had last been there, both in the way the stadium looked and the way it played. While the exterior, for the most part, remained the same, one hundred and eighteen obstructive steel columns reinforcing each tier of the stadium's grandstand were removed. When Shea Stadium was built in 1964, it was the first stadium in the major leagues that did not have these annoying poles. Now, twelve years and $160 million later, Yankee Stadium too had pristine sight lines.

Another major change was that the original roof, with its iconic façade, was removed. However, the architects were able to create a replica of the façade to sit on top of the new scoreboard and stretch across the bleachers. The new scoreboard, which was huge compared to the original scoreboard, was the first in the majors capable of showing instant replays. It was not in color and it was nothing compared to today's high-definition scoreboards, but in 1976, the shades of gray replays were new and exciting.

The stadium's capacity was changed from 65,010 to 57,545.

The hardest part of moving back to the new, renovated Yankee Stadium was remembering where things had been before the renovation took place. The changes were so absolute that many historians refuse to consider it the same stadium before and after the renovation.

"The changes were such, that I could never figure out what used to be where when I was standing in a certain place in the new stadium," Appel said. "They really gutted it and completely rebuilt it. I would be in some spot below the stands and I would just stop and ask myself 'What used to be here?' and I could never figure it out."

Some things were removed that most of the fans didn't even know about. During the renovation process, a super-secret electrical room, which was more like a vault that was underground under second base, was bulldozed and destroyed.

"Col. Ruppert (the Yankees owner who built the original Yankee Stadium) and his partner Col. Til Huston, installed a vault under second base containing the necessary equipment to stage boxing matches above," Appel writes in his article, *Secrets of Yankee Stadium*. "The most famous of course, would be the historic Joe Louis-Max Schmeling rematch—the one Louis won in the first round."

As Appel writes in his book, *Pinstripe Empire*, it was another vault entirely that was the saddest casualty of the renovation. Back in 1903, when the New York Yankees were still the New York Highlanders, a safe was installed in the players' clubhouse at Hilltop Park in upper Manhattan. Player names from that team were still visible on the drawers of the safe. When the team moved to the Polo Grounds, the safe made the trip, as it did when the Yankees moved into their new stadium in the Bronx in 1923. The safe made yet another move in 1946 when the Yankees rebuilt their clubhouse. There it remained until the final day of the 1973 season.

"It never made it to Shea and disappeared forever," Appel wrote, noting that it was not part of the large number of things a collector named Bert Sugar was allowed to take from the stadium and then sell. "It had just vanished in the demolition, its historical value never realized."

What was also exciting was the brand of baseball the Yankees were playing back in the Bronx. Finally with a home to call their own once again, the Yankees won ninety-seven games in 1976—drawing a league-best 2,012,434 fans. After defeating the Kansas City Royals in an exciting American League Championship Series, the Yankees advanced to their first World Series since 1964. When they got there, however, they ran head-on into the Big Red Machine, which swept the Yankees in four games. The seed had been planted.

By the spring of 1977, the Yankees were not going to settle for anything less than a championship, and that is exactly what they got. On the strength of Reggie Jackson's bat and great pitching, the Yankees won back-to-back World Series titles. The Yankees—and Yankee Stadium—were really back.

Today, with the Yankees playing in Yankee Stadium number three, fans tend to have revisionist history about the old ballparks in the Bronx.

"When the refurbished Yankee Stadium closed after 2008, most people were saying how they preferred the original one and really missed it a lot, and that the remodeled one was inferior to that," Appel said. "The reality wasn't that at all. When we moved in in 1976, people loved it and loved it a lot more than the original one, but eventually nostalgia won out and people thought that the original stadium was a lot better than it was. Nostalgia does that. People old enough remember and miss Ebbets Field, and Ebbets Field was a miserable place to be. It was small, the sightlines were bad, and it just wasn't a good experience—but everyone remembers it fondly now."

Kind of like Shea Stadium.

• • • •

While the Yankees found immediate success following their stay in Queens, the transition to being home was not as smooth for the New York Giants. They were not returning to hallowed ground, or the scene of past glories. Instead, they were going to play in a state that was different than the one that had long been depicted on their helmets. The New York Giants were no longer playing in New York. There were many adjustments to be made. For one thing, the "NY" was taken off of the Giants helmets, out of respect for the fact that they were now playing in New Jersey. For many years, the Giants had a lowercase "ny," only to change it to a capital "NY" for the 1975 season at Shea. From 1976 through 1999, the helmets had "GIANTS" written across both sides. The lowercase "ny" didn't return to the helmets until 2000.

That first year at Giants Stadium, things were less than perfect for the team and its owner, Wellington Mara, as the Giants went just 3-11 overall.

"When we first moved into Giants Stadium, I remember him being hung in effigy from the upper deck," said Giants co-owner John Mara of his father. "It was our time in the wilderness from 1974-1980, where we didn't make the playoffs and finished last on a number of occasions. It was really the darkest period of our history."

It took more than ten years since leaving Shea Stadium for the Giants to reach the Super Bowl. By 1986, the Giants had not only become a respectable NFL team, but also they were the most powerful in the league. Their 14-2 record preceded two dominating playoff victories, and a trip to Super Bowl XXI in Pasadena. The Giants made the most of their opportunity, rolling over the Denver Broncos to win the franchise's first Super Bowl title and first championship since 1956. Finally, Wellington Mara had restored the Giants to greatness.

"There's no question about it, being in Pasadena in January of 1987 and watching [my father] accept the Lombardi Trophy will always be one of the great memories of my life because that ended that long, long championship drought," John Mara said. "We felt we were back as a franchise and were to be respected. To see that happiness he had at that point in time will stick with me forever. For those of us who remember, the darker days make the success that much more gratifying when you achieve it."

Two years later, the Washington Redskins took the field against the Denver Broncos in San Diego for Super Bowl XXIII. Washington's quarterback, Doug Williams, was the same Doug Williams who quarterbacked his Grambling Tigers to victory in 1975 at Shea Stadium.

Thirteen years after Williams made his last appearance in Flushing, he dominated the Broncos, scoring thirty-five points on eighteen plays in the second quarter alone. For the game, Williams completed eighteen of twenty-nine passes, four of which were for touchdowns, and the Redskins cruised to a 42-10 victory. Williams was named the Super Bowl MVP for his efforts, proving that his legendary college coach— Eddie Robinson—wasn't always correct. Not *everything* "worth a damn" has to go through New York.

• • • •

Beginning in 1976, the Mets and Jets returned to a sense of normalcy, which gave way to the reality that they were playing in a stadium that—at only twelve years old—was beginning to feel more than a bit outdated. After witnessing championship games for the Mets and Jets within the first five years of its existence, Shea Stadium fell into significant disrepair in the years following 1975. As the Mets played worse and worse, and New York City fell into deeper and deeper financial straits, Shea Stadium was largely ignored.

"Ghosts peopled 126th Street and Roosevelt Avenue," author Curt Smith wrote. "New York, New York was again a Yankees, Yankees town."

It wasn't just the losing, however; it was the total and utter plunge of the team and for the building that it called home.

After finishing in third place in 1976, the bottom fell out for the Mets—and Shea Stadium—as the team finished dead last in the National League East in 1977, 1978, and 1979.

"Nothing was more depressing than seeing that ballpark and seeing that team in 1979," said Mets broadcaster Howie Rose. "I know there were worse seasons, but to me that was the low point in the history of the franchise. New York City was broke, Shea Stadium was a municipal building, and it was in ridiculous disrepair for a place that was only fifteen years old.

"Nothing had been painted, everything looked old and worn and shoddy, and it was just such an unfortunate juxtaposition from the memories I had from its apex just ten years earlier when the Mets won the 1969 World Series. At that time it was capital of the baseball world and the capital of my life, really. To see the way it looked in 1979 was tremendously depressing. It just hurt. Knowing what the Mets had meant to this town and what that ballpark was like in the late '60s and early '70s—when the Mets absolutely owned New York—it was really painful."

Those painful years for the stadium were also extremely painful for the Mets—and many of their players. For one, Ed Kranepool—an original member of the Mets—had had enough by the end of that 1979 season, when the Mets went a pitiful 28-53 at Shea Stadium. Kranepool insists he could have hung on for a few more years, but was very unhappy with the way he was being treated by Mets manager Joe Torre. Torre had taken over as a player-manager in 1977 and was the manager of the team from 1978 through 1981.

While Torre in later years would go on to win multiple championships and be revered as one of the greatest managers in the history of New York—for the Yankees—in 1979 he had not yet earned those stripes.

"The only reason my numbers diminished at the end of my career was because of Joe Torre and the fact that he stopped playing me," Kranepool said. "You can't play once a week and expect to do well. He didn't manage very well with the Mets. He really didn't know what he was doing. But he really shortened my career just due to inactivity. You can rust away."

For pitcher Jerry Koosman, there was one really big day in the sun before the dark days of the Mets arrived. Ironically, however, his day in the sun began with a personal dark day—his father's death in the spring of 1976.

"To tell you the truth, I don't remember 1974 and 1975 that well, but it's 1976 that I really remember," Koosman said. "My father died that spring, toward the end of spring training. It was like his spirit was with me the whole year and my concentration level was just tremendous. I was never able to reach that concentration level again after that year. It was very special, being the first year that I won twenty games."

Following that magical season for Koosman, during which he went 21-10 and finished second in the National League Cy Young voting, things began a downward slide for the Mets. It was not a long slide, because on June 15, 1977, it went from a slide to a massacre—"The Midnight Massacre," as fans and media would call it.

On that one day, Mets chairman M. Donald Grant traded the heart and soul of the Mets when he dealt away the face of the franchise, Tom Seaver, and slugger Dave Kingman. The trades—especially the Seaver deal—were due to money issues and Grant felt he could get some good young talent in exchange for the stars. Although he got young players, the talent was debatable, and Shea Stadium soon became known as "Grant's Tomb."

Matlack was one of many Mets who were not pleased with the direction in which the team was heading. After a third-straight All-Star season in 1976, winning seventeen games, Matlack—like the Mets—struggled in 1977.

"It wasn't that we went into a ballgame not expecting support," Matlack said of the offensive support he and his fellow pitchers were getting, "but we knew if we didn't give up much, we didn't need much."

By the end of 1977, Matlack's tenure with the Mets was over.

"It was somewhat frustrating," Matlack said. "There were some people in the front office who thought I was a rebel, stirring the pot and causing trouble. In reality, all I wanted to see was an effort to put a better product on the field. When they traded Tom, it seemed to not be about baseball, but more about extraneous things, and that was a little bit upsetting. I was next in that boat and I think they almost wanted me to say that I wanted to be traded, which I never did."

Matlack did, however, break the golden rule of Major League Baseball, which he had been told about many years earlier.

"The kiss of death for me was buying a new house," Matlack joked. "The day I finished the last project, which was a screened-in porch, I finished painting the thing and when I was in the basement cleaning the brushes, I got a call from Joe McDonald who told me I was traded to Texas."

For the remaining players (such as Koosman), losing key members, such as Seaver, Matlack, Kingman, Staub, and others, definitely affected the team's resolve. As did playing to a near empty Shea Stadium, which saw its attendance drop to under one million for the first time ever in 1979.

"There's nothing better than a full stadium and having enough talent to be winning," said Koosman, who lost a league-high twenty games in 1977. "Things had really slowed down for us. There were some player changes and a bunch of little things. I just don't know what the reasons were, but we just weren't able to win."

Koosman's shift from going 21-10 to going 8-20 was staggering and a sign less about his abilities and more about his team's ineptitude.

After one more dreadful year with the Mets, Koosman himself would mercifully be traded to the Minnesota Twins for a minor-leaguer and a player to be named later. In his first year pitching for the Twins, Koosman won twenty games.

One year after Koosman re-established himself as one of the finest pitchers in the game, another former Met—relief pitcher Tug McGraw—was helping his Philadelphia team to a world championship.

McGraw pitched in all five games of the 1980 National League Championship Series against the Houston Astros, earning two saves. He then appeared in four of the six games of the 1980 World Series against the Kansas City Royals. McGraw struck out ten batters in $7^2/3$ innings and was on the mound when the Phillies clinched the title. At a victory rally the next day, McGraw jubilantly summed up the championship for the Phillies fans, who had waited ninety-seven years for a World Series title.

"All through baseball history, Philadelphia has had to take a back seat to New York City," McGraw proclaimed. "Well, New York City can take this world championship and stick it, because we're number one!"

In later years, McGraw expressed remorse regarding his comments toward New York, and would come to Shea Stadium from time to time over the years to be with the Mets fans—who he always stated he loved. McGraw was inducted into the Mets Hall of Fame in 1993 and died in 2004 over complications from a brain tumor. The Mets played the 2004 season with the words "Ya Gotta Believe" embroidered on their left shoulders in McGraw's memory.

The same season that McGraw was leading the Phillies to a championship, the Payson family sold the New York Mets. The new owners—Nelson Doubleday and Fred Wilpon—immediately started making major changes to Shea. The stadium was only sixteen years old, but it was an old sixteen.

The building's original wooden seats were replaced by: red (upper deck), green (mezzanine), blue (loge), and orange (field level) plastic seats. The blue and orange exterior tiles, which gave Shea Stadium an unmistakable look, were now outdated and were removed. A picnic area and left-field bleachers were added.

One year later, the Mets established a Mets Hall of Fame. The first two inductees were Casey Stengel and Joan Payson. That same year, a giant top hat with an apple inside was built beyond the center field fence. Every time a Mets player hit a home run, the apple would rise up out of the hat. The home run apple has become known as one of the most beloved aspects of the Mets' franchise.

In 1982, the stadium that was the first to have an electronic scoreboard installed a giant DiamondVision video display screen in left-center field. The screen was thirty-five feet, eight inches wide by twenty-six feet, three inches high.

In April of 1984, while preparing for an estate sale at the home of the late Mets owner Joan Payson, two nationally historic treasures were found in the compartment of a table. The first was a manuscript of President Abraham Lincoln's last public address. The other was an autographed poster of poet Walt Whitman, as well as a letter from Whitman to Joan Payson's grandfather.

• • • •

Like the Mets, the Jets struggled mightily for the remainder of the 1970s. Top players began to leave Queens, either on their own, or by trade.

Following the 1975 season, the Jets' best player—John Riggins— went for the big money in Washington, signing a four-year, $1.5 million contract. The annual salary of $375,000 per season dwarfed the $75,000 he had earned in his final year with the Jets. Riggins had a stellar career with the Redskins, leading them to the Super Bowl XVII title in 1983 and earning himself the MVP trophy with a Super Bowl–record 166 rushing yards on a Super Bowl-record thirty-eight rushing attempts. He also had one reception for fifteen yards, giving him more yards on his own than the entire Miami Dolphins team gained in front of 103,000 people at the Rose Bowl in Pasadena.

One of Riggins's teammates on Washington's championship team was his former teammate, Rich Caster, the Jets' leading receiver for much of the 1970s. During training camp leading up to the 1978 season, Caster—the three-time Pro Bowler for the Jets—had been traded to the Houston Oilers. While he was shocked at first, Caster settled in very nicely in Houston, reaching the playoffs in each of three seasons with the Oilers. He never had the personal, statistical success he had in New York, but he enjoyed his time much more in Houston—if for no other reason than the fact that he was on a winning team.

"That's where my fondest memories really are," Caster said of his time playing in Houston. "We went to the AFC Conference Championship all three years I was there. I played with a lot of great ballplayers there, and it was that experience—and those three years— that were my favorite years as a player. They were my most fun years. I did have some years in New York where I was on top of my game and I can certainly smile about. But in terms of good feelings and team spirit and the thought that we could win any game we were playing in, for me that was in Houston."

Despite enjoying much of his time playing with the Jets, he has little love when he thinks back to Shea Stadium. He does, however, remember very clearly the first time he was exposed to Shea when he first reported to the Jets after being drafted out of Jackson State. He also remembers making his first receptions at Shea, catching his first passes from his sixty-eight-year-old "quarterback."

"It was the place I came when I arrive in New York. I arrived at LaGuardia Airport and met [Jets head coach] Weeb Ewbank in the parking lot of Shea Stadium," Caster said. "He was throwing me passes and I didn't think he had enough arm to do it, but he was doing it. It was really a start for me. That's my first impression of Shea Stadium, catching passes in the parking lot from Weeb Ewbank. Still, even with that, it doesn't rank as one of the top places in my life where I can say 'Wow, do I miss that.'"

Caster, like many of his Jets teammates, associate Shea Stadium with a losing mentality. By the time he arrived in 1970, the Jets' winning culture was heading downward and Caster never experienced a winning season in New York.

"I think a lot about the unfortunate years that the Jets had and that it's a place where we didn't have enough success that would make me miss Shea Stadium," Caster said. "I don't miss Shea like some people might miss Yankee Stadium, or some of those other stadiums like Ebbets Field. The idea that Shea is gone, I don't think a lot of the people who I played with regret it being replaced by something else. It kind of held the memories of a lot of failed seasons for the Jets. It was just not a great place to be and doesn't find itself in my memory as a place that I can say 'I had a great time there.' It was where we had to play."

In 1976, the Jets managed to win just three games during the entire season, with only one of those victories coming at Shea Stadium. That season would be the last that Joe Namath would spend in New York. Broadway Joe signed with the Los Angeles Rams leading up to the 1977 season, hoping a change of scenery would help turn back the clock.

Unfortunately for Namath, the clock was striking midnight. Injuries and interceptions limited Namath to playing only a handful of games for the Rams, and the quarterback called it quits after the season.

The clock was about to strike midnight for the Jets at Shea Stadium at around the same time. Not long after seeing the carpetbagging Yankees and Giants bolt from Shea Stadium following the 1975 season, the Jets started to have similar intentions. Much like the Giants felt like second-class citizens in Yankee Stadium, the Jets always felt as if they were the stepchild of Shea Stadium. Due to an agreement signed in 1961 by the original owners of the New York Titans (who would become the Jets), the Mets had sole rights to play at Shea Stadium until their season was over. The Jets could not play a home game most years for the first three to four weeks of the season. By 1977, they had had enough of what they felt was an outdated agreement. Still, the Jets' lease at Shea did not run out until following the 1983 season.

The Jets announced that instead of waiting for the Mets to finish their season at Shea each year, that they were going to go to play two September games across the river at Giants Stadium. This enraged New York City and its mayor, Ed Koch, who sued the team. The two sides ended the litigation process and New York City agreed to allow the Jets to play the two September games in New Jersey for the remaining seven years of their lease.

The Jets and their owner, Leon Hess, fully planned to renew their lease at Shea Stadium and remain in New York, assuming that the lease could be re-worked to include some new provisions for the Jets. For example, Hess was hoping that Shea Stadium could be reconfigured to add seating and increase its capacity for football games and that the Jets would be able to receive some of the moneys from stadium parking—which had always gone to New York City. Mayor Koch stonewalled Hess and the Jets, however, and in late 1983 the Jets announced that they would follow the Giants to New Jersey. As more than a little dig at the team, at the end of the team's final home game—a 34-7 loss to the Pittsburgh Steelers—the Shea Stadium scoreboard referred to the team as the "N.J. Jets."

After the Jets moved out of Shea Stadium following the 1983 football season, the Mets took over complete operation of the stadium and retrofitted it for exclusive baseball use.

• • • •

No season at Shea—other than 1969—is remembered as fondly as 1986.

In 1984, the Mets came seemingly out of nowhere to battle with the Chicago Cubs right down to the wire for the National League East crown. The Mets had been energized by rookie pitcher Dwight Gooden and young slugger Darryl Strawberry, they had traded for star power when they dealt for Keith Hernandez midway through the previous year, and they had a new, young, popular-with-the-players manager named Davey Johnson. He was, in fact, the same Davey Johnson that sent a fly ball to Cleon Jones for the final out of the 1969 World Series. Nevertheless, the Mets fell short at the end of 1984, although they won ninety games for the first time since 1969, when they had won one hundred games.

Prior to the 1985 campaign, the Mets made another splash, trading for all-star catcher Gary Carter from the Montreal Expos. Along with Carter came a boldness to the team—some would say cockiness—that led to more and more wins. However, ninety-eight wins would not be enough to win the division crown in 1985. Most years, ninety-eight wins would have been just fine, but not this year. The St. Louis Cardinals were able to win 101 games, and hold off the Mets during a late-season head-to-head series. The Mets would have to wait one more year.

When that year finally arrived, there seemed little doubt about the outcome. After beginning the season with a 2-3 record, the Mets exploded to win eighteen of their next nineteen games. By the end of August, the Mets were ahead by so many games that clinching the division was merely a formality. On the blue left-field fence at Shea Stadium, big bold letters spelled out: "A September to Remember." By the time it was all over the Mets would win 108 regular-season games.

After a nail-biting National League Championship Series win over the Houston Astros, the Mets took on the Boston Red Sox in the

World Series. Things could not have started worse. The Red Sox took the first two games at Shea Stadium, putting the happy ending the Mets and their fans had been counting on in great jeopardy. After taking two of three games in Boston, the Mets returned to Shea Stadium for a contest that would come to be known simply as Game Six.

Trailing 5-3 in the bottom of the tenth inning, the Mets' season was on life support. When the first two batters were retired, the team started to flatline.

Mets third base coach Bud Harrelson looked over toward the Red Sox dugout and saw his old buddy and possibly the greatest pitcher to ever climb the mound at Shea Stadium, Tom Seaver. Seaver was a member of the Red Sox roster in 1986, but was inactive for the World Series because he was hurt.

"He was sitting in front of the camera well next to the dugout, so he wasn't too far away from me at third base," Harrelson recalled. "When we got two outs and then when Carter got two strikes on him, I looked over at Tom and he put his thumb up to his ear with his pinkie out, basically saying 'I'll call you' because it was about to be mayhem [for the Red Sox]. That didn't happen."

Instead, in a flash, everything else happened. Gary Carter singled. Kevin Mitchell singled. Ray Knight singled, scoring Carter and sending Mitchell to third base.

Standing at third base to greet Mitchell was Harrelson. Mitchell was ninety feet from scoring what seemed moments earlier to be an impossible tying run. Harrelson reminded Mitchell to be aware for a pitch in the dirt.

"You told me, you told me," Kevin Mitchell barked back at Harrelson.

But Harrelson, who was standing just about fifty feet from where he stood when the Mets clinched their first world championship, had a feeling something great was going to happen with Mookie Wilson at the plate.

"Bob Stanley had just come in and [Rich] Gedman—who was a good hitter—was only an average catcher," Harrelson said. "I said it and then was hoping for it, because we needed it."

Sure enough, Stanley uncorked a pitch that got away from Rich Gedman and rolled all the way to the backstop, allowing Mitchell to score the tying run. Knight went to second base on the play. Unbelievably, the Mets were a base hit—or error—away from an impossible victory. Little did everyone know at the time, the Red Sox locker room was prepared for a champagne celebration—complete with plastic over all of the lockers. It would have been Boston's first title since 1918.

But the game was now tied and the potential winning run was standing on second base for the Mets.

What happened next has gone down in history as one of the most watched—and re-watched—plays in World Series history. Mookie Wilson hit what appeared to be a simple ground ball to first base. But simple turned quickly into ever-lasting. The legendary Vin Scully made a call for the ages on a play that was meant for the ages.

Little roller up along first, behind the bag, it gets through Buckner, here comes Knight and the Mets win it!

"I always said that I think [Buckner] looked up to see where Stanley was. It was kind of an easy play, except for who was running," Harrelson said. "I don't think Stanley was going to beat Mookie to first base, but that doesn't mean we win, because I can't send Knight. But I was way down the line, because that is what I do with a guy coming to third. I'm either going to hold him or send him."

Then, the unthinkable happened—the ball bounced between Buckner's legs, under his mitt, and rolled into right field.

"When [Buckner] missed the ball, I was actually leading Knight running to home plate, so I had to slow down to let him score."

The Mets had somehow survived to play another day.

"We didn't win it that night, we just didn't lose it. But that's one you will never forget. It doesn't happen like that very often," Harrelson said.

Two nights later, the Mets erased an early 3-0 Boston lead and went on to win their second world championship in team history.

The man who was on the mound to close out the clinching game for the Mets was Jesse Orosco—the "player to be named later" when New York traded Jerry Koosman to Minnesota.

"That's great, two good left-handers," Koosman said with a hearty laugh. "I was happy for Jesse, he carried on the energy. It's amazing how things turn out looking back in history."

• • • •

As the years went on, the key people from that 1975 season at Shea went in very different and very interesting directions.

Following his time as public relations director with the Yankees, Marty Appel went on to start a sports management company, work for Major League Baseball, become an award-winning author, and found Marty Appel Public Relations, which is based in New York.

However, perhaps there is no aspect of Appel's life that is as interesting as what he has done over the years for the National Baseball Hall of Fame and Museum. Appel has had the opportunity to contribute his writing to dozens of the Hall of Fame plaques that adorn the walls in Cooperstown—mostly from the late 1970s and 1980s.

"I've always been close to the people at the Hall of Fame and I was one of the people who they would send a draft to and if I had any suggestions; a lot of them were incorporated into the plaques," Appel said. "If I walk past a plaque from that era now and I see one that was mine, that's a really good feeling."

Although he always enjoyed being able to contribute his writings to the plaques, there was one specific one that he calls his favorite.

"My best one was Bill Veeck," Appel said, referring to the former owner. "It was hard to put on the plaque that he sent a midget up to bat. That really doesn't get you in the Hall of Fame, although it can keep you out. But I put on the last line of his plaque 'a champion of the little guy.'"

Appel looks back fondly on his days working for the Yankees, and the time he and the team spent on "the road" at Shea Stadium. Although it was an odd time for the team, Appel wishes more people would give the 1974 and 1975 Yankees the credit they deserve.

"I have some regret that it's kind of forgotten," Appel said.

• • • •

Robert Moses—although gone—has never really been forgotten. Following the scathing 1974 biography on Moses's life—*The Power Broker*, written by Robert Caro—Moses's public life was over. He tried desperately to regain some kind of power, but to no avail.

In late August of 1974, weeks before Caro's book was published, the eighty-six-year-old Moses released a 3,500-word rebuttal that said the book was "full of mistakes, unsupported charges, nasty, baseless personalities, and random haymakers thrown at just about everybody in public life." However, Moses was already exposed for the bully he was and all of the reviews of Caro's book were high praise.

David Halberstam called *The Power Broker* "surely the greatest book ever written about a city." *New York* magazine said it was "the most absorbing, detailed, instructive, provocative book ever published about the making and raping of modern New York City and environs and the man who did it."

In one of the last interviews Moses gave, the old man appeared on PBS Channel Thirteen in New York. He was defiant and racist. When challenged on the increasing movements against urban displacement he responded, "Let's be sensible. How do you visualize the area that we cleared out for the Fordham expansion downtown? They needed the space. Now I ask you, what was that neighborhood? It was a Puerto Rican slum. Do you remember it? Yeah, well I lived there for many years and it was the worst slum in New York. And you want to leave it there?"

Moses spent his final days in solitude, swimming and probably planning in his mind new things to build. His work—much of which bears his name—is littered throughout the New York City Metropolitan area. On Long Island, the Robert Moses State Park and Robert Moses Causeway remain. There are schools named for him, statues of his likeness, and playgrounds named in his honor. That might have been his biggest positive—by the time he left office, he had built 658 playgrounds in New York City alone. He died on Long Island at the age of ninety-two in 1981.

The man who teamed up with Moses in many ways, William Shea, for years maintained his large Manhattan law firm. He never lost

Today, Shea Stadium is remembered in the parking lot of Citi Field.
Courtesy of Greg Goodman/AdventuresofaGoodMan.com

his love for the Mets or the building that was named for him. Each Opening Day, Shea would present a wreath of flowers to the manager at home plate.

"Shea retained his interest in sports, and was considered in 1965 to succeed Ford Frick as the baseball commissioner," David Margolick wrote in the *New York Times*. "He helped the city fight to keep the Jets in Shea Stadium, and maintained his interest in the Mets, appearing [as late as 1991] in a wheelchair for the induction of Cleon Jones into the team's Hall of Fame."

A few months after that ceremony, in October of 1991, Shea died at the age of eighty-four. However, the man responsible for delivering the Mets to New York lives on at Citi Field. The Shea Bridge proudly sits in right-center field, carrying fans from one end of the stadium to the other. Shea's name is also hanging next to the team's retired numbers beyond the left-field fence.

• • • •

The Polo Grounds died much earlier than Moses or Shea. Following the Mets' and Jets' fleeing of the dilapidated old stadium, the stadium was torn down beginning in 1964. A public housing project, the Polo Grounds Towers, was erected in 1968.

However, the Polo Grounds was back in the news in 2015 when New York City restored one of its last remnants. The Brush Stairway, which ran down Coogan's Bluff to the stadium, roughly where Edgecombe Avenue runs today, was restored to be as good as new. The staircase at one time led to a ticket booth built by the Giants in 1913. In 2015, the stairway leads to nowhere. On the landing, about halfway down is an inscription: "The John T. Brush Stairway Presented by the New York Giants." The stairway was built to honor Brush, the Giants owner who died the year before, in 1912.

The renovated stairway cost $950,000. Of that, the New York Giants football team donated $200,000, the Mets and Yankees each donated $100,000, and the Jets, the San Francisco Giants, and Major

League Baseball each donated $50,000. The Manhattan borough president's office paid the rest.

. . . .

Two decades after leaving Washington in disgrace, Richard Nixon could often be spotted in the field box section of Shea Stadium taking in a game. During the mid-1980s, Nixon followed the Mets closely. In 1985, he was asked to serve as mediator when the major league umpires asked for money to officiate the new, longer postseason. He ended up giving the umpires a 40 percent raise.

In 1987, following a game at Shea, Nixon appeared on the Mets televised postgame show, lauding about some of the team's talent.

"It's the most exciting thing to watch him hit," Nixon said of Darryl Strawberry. "When he hits one out, there's no question about it."

Nixon went on to name some former presidents to his Presidential All-Star Baseball team. He thought perhaps Woodrow Wilson could start at first base.

"Eisenhower could have played second, but I think he would have been better as an outfielder," said Nixon, enjoying the game he and broadcaster Fran Healey were playing. As for shortstop, he replied, "maybe Madison, because he was very short."

His closer? "Maybe Theodore Roosevelt. He was a leader-type who could get up there and stomp around the mound. Particularly I think he would be a good reliever because he would frighten the batter."

Finally, Nixon was asked to give his opinion about the fact that some Russian historians feel that their country had, in fact, invented baseball.

"Well, you know they claim to have invented a lot of things," Nixon said with a hearty laugh.

. . . .

The Yankees did return to Shea Stadium for one more home game on April 15, 1998. Following the collapse of a beam at Yankee Stadium, which destroyed several rows of seats, the Yankees—led by their manager Joe Torre—borrowed Shea for one afternoon. For this game, the Yankees used the visitor's clubhouse and their opponent, the California Angels, were relegated to the smelly, old Jets locker room.

During the game, former Mets great Darryl Strawberry—now a member of the Yankees—blasted a home run. The big apple started to rise, flashing the Mets logo. After making it up halfway, the apple was stopped and returned back into its large top hat. The fans enjoyed a good laugh.

Two years later, the Yankees returned to Shea once again. This time, it was not Strawberry who returned wearing a Yankees' uniform, but two other former Mets stars—Dwight Gooden and David Cone—who returned to Shea Stadium for one last act. Gooden and Cone were members of the 2000 American League champions who were taking on the Mets in the World Series—the Mets' first trip to the Fall Classic since 1986. Although Gooden never made it into the Series, and Cone pitched in just a third of an inning, the duo—along with their manager Joe Torre—got the chance to celebrate once again at Shea.

More than twenty-five years after grounding into four straight double plays as a member of the Mets, Torre was carried off of the Shea Stadium field with his fourth World Series title in five years. It would be the last World Series that Torre would win, and the last World Series that Shea Stadium would host.

• • • •

In the summer of 2006, it was clear that something was about to change in and around Shea Stadium. As the Mets marched toward what they hoped was another trip to the World Series, trucks and activity started to hustle and bustle in the parking lot beyond the stadium. The Mets would fall short of their goals, losing to the St. Louis Cardinals in Game Seven of the National League Championship Series. However, in November of 2006, ground was broken on what would become their new home.

Throughout the 2007 season, a brand-new stadium began to rise just feet from Shea Stadium. By Opening Day 2008—the final season

Thirty-three years after the 1975 season, Shea Stadium met its demise.
Courtesy of Brett Topel

at Shea—the entire structure of what would come to be known as Citi Field was in place. Following an extremely difficult end of the season for the Mets in 2008—during which the team blew a big September lead for the second year in a row to fall short of the playoffs—Shea Stadium had completed its baseball journey. The last batter to ever step to the plate was Ryan Church.

"It wasn't easy to see Shea go, but it was harder to see it in disrepair than it was to see it torn down, to tell you the truth," said Howie Rose. "I savored every last minute of my last day in the ballpark. The emotions that day were complex and melancholy and sad and celebratory and devastating all at once—and that's a bad mix. That's a combustible mix. So it was not a pleasant day, and yet I had to savor every last bit of it. After everyone had left, I walked around the infield by myself and I just looked up at every nook and cranny of the ballpark and tried to soak it all in, because that's where my life was spent from 1964 through 2008."

It was an emotional day for Rose, who—like many Mets fans—were not looking forward to seeing the old stadium torn down. Following the loss to the Marlins, the Mets held a Shea Goodbye ceremony, as many players from the franchise's history returned to touch home plate for one last time. So many were from that 1975 season. Tom Seaver, Ed Kranepool, Jerry Koosman, Rusty Staub, Bud Harrelson, and even Yogi Berra were all there.

As the crowd roared, Seaver made his way to the Shea Stadium mound for one more pitch—to Mike Piazza. Following the pitch, the two embraced as Louis Armstrong's "What a Wonderful World" blared from the outdated Shea sound system. As the two made their way off the field through the center-field fence, their exit song was "In My Life" by, who else, the Beatles.

"I used to fantasize about being the guy who got the hit to win the game, and later to be the guy who called the hit to win the game," said Rose, who served as the emcee for the final ceremony at Shea. "Having realized that dream, I couldn't let go of that place, but I knew when I left that day, I didn't want to come back until it was all down. I did not want to see it in its skeletal state, I did not want to see the rubble, I did not want to see my memories reduced to dust."

For one of the most popular players in Mets' history, saying good-bye to Shea was bittersweet, knowing that there were better things on the horizon for the team and its fans.

"A lot of us were there for the last game at Shea and a lot of people said 'we like Shea Stadium,' but I told them that they liked the memories," said Bud Harrelson, who played for the Mets from 1965 through 1977, coached the team in the 1980s, and was its manager from 1990-91. "Shea Stadium was obsolete just a few years after it was built. I called it the last dinosaur. I enjoyed playing at Shea very much, but I was also very happy that the Mets got a new ballpark."

Of all of the players who came back to say good-bye to the big ballpark in Flushing, there were no Yankees from the 1974 and

1975 seasons. In fact, in all of the farewell fanfare surrounding Shea in its final months, the Yankees' short stay as co-tenants remained unacknowledged.

"When Shea Stadium closed in 2008, there were a lot of remembrances on television and in print about great things that had taken place there," said Appel, noting the inclusion of many of Shea's highlights, including the Beatles concerts. "Nowhere were the 162 Yankees games that were there. It was kind of like gone and forgotten."

• • • •

On a chilly winter day in late 2008, Josh Bernstein—a friend of mine since college and currently a senior executive at the Major League Baseball Network—invited me to attend a tour with him of Citi Field while it was still under construction. We donned hard hats—not the greatest look for either of us—and were led around the new stadium, taking in all its glory. It was simply amazing to see the new home of the Mets, up close and personal.

At one point of the tour, we were led up a staircase not far down the third-base line. We climbed the stairs to a small landing, and that's when we saw it. It was as if we were witnessing the death of a friend. There was Shea Stadium—even though it was no longer Shea Stadium. The field had been bulldozed, and heavy machinery, dumpsters, and piles of debris took up residence in what was once the infield. The hulking scoreboard in right-center field had been torn down and the video board in left-center field—which would always be known to a certain generation of Mets fans as DiamondVision—was gone. The seats were no longer there. In fact, the field level and most of the loge sections were completely gone. The mezzanine and upper deck sections were being torn down as we stood and watched. Everything that made Shea Stadium Shea Stadium was gone.

"I can vividly remember the feeling that day," Bernstein said. "Entire sections were being smashed in front of our eyes. It was a surreal scene. As I watched, specific memories of games I went to sitting in those exact sections flashed in my memory. It was something I felt we shouldn't have been allowed to see. Perhaps we weren't actually supposed be there at all, but—in retrospect—I'm glad we were."

It was impossible to believe this was the same place where I too had witnessed so many great baseball games. I had been there with my grandfather, with my parents and sister and uncles and cousins and countless friends. I had been there with my wife and with my son. But I would never be there again.

Forty years after the Mets, Yankees, Giants, and Jets all shared Shea Stadium—and seven years since I had witnessed Shea being ripped apart—I climbed that same staircase once again in 2015. I looked out from the landing and saw, not a mangled ballpark, but a sea of cars where Shea Stadium had once stood. I remember saying out loud to my son, "Shea was right there." He indicated that I had mentioned that before. It was at that point that I realized it wasn't him I was trying to remind.

ACKNOWLEDGMENTS

I HAVE ALWAYS FELT THAT writing a book is not really about writing, but more about going on a personal journey. When you get to your final destination, you can only hope the stories that you have to share live up to the journey itself.

I want to first thank my editor, Julie Ganz, and her entire team at Sports Publishing. Julie's support of this project was absolute, and no author could ever ask for anything more. Without Mark Rosenman, however, I would have never found Julie in the first place. Mark, for me, it was definitely "worth it."

I had the great fortune to speak to many first-person sources for this book—each gave me a unique and outstanding perspective to help shape my writings. They are: Giants co-owner John Mara; former Yankees PR director Marty Appel; former Yankees' manager Bill Virdon; former Mets players Jerry Koosman, Jon Matlack, Ed Kranepool, and Bud Harrelson; former Super Bowl MVP and Grambling football great Doug Williams; former Jets tight end Richard Caster; New York Supreme Court Justice Rolando Acosta; and NBC News legend Carl Stern. I want to give a special thank-you to Mets broadcaster, team historian, and friend, Howie Rose, as well as former Mets head groundskeeper Pete Flynn.

Thank you to: My mentor Jack Heidenry, even if he doesn't realize he is my mentor; John Horne at the Baseball Hall of Fame and Museum in Cooperstown; Midge Ure, for graciously allowing me to reprint his fine lyrics; Adam Schefter, Kenny Zore, and Larry Ross for all of your help; Dr. Jean-Marc Juhel for all of your encouragement; my brother EP for your unwavering support; JB and Big Stein for sharing your great memories; Melissa, Jason, Derek, Kayla, Abigale, David, Cooper, and Quinn for always being there; Ellen and Steve for your unconditional love and support; and my mom and dad, the two people who I strive most to emulate—I could not ask for more loving and supportive parents, and I know that I am only able to do what I do because of what they have given to me; William, Rosie, and Pogo, for all you do; Oliver, who has become a young man before my eyes and is in every way a true friend; and Lily, whose big eyes simply energize any room. You will always be my princess. Finally, to Emily, I can't imagine not having you by my side, and luckily, I don't have to.

Sources

First-Person Interviews
(alphabetically)

Justice Rolando Acosta, Marty Appel, Richard Caster, Pete Flynn, Bud Harrelson, Jerry Koosman, Ed Kranepool, John Mara, Jon Matlack, Chico Resch, Howie Rose, Carl Stern, Bill Virdon, and Doug Williams.

Books

Appel, Marty. *Pinstripe Empire: The New York Yankees from Before the Babe to After the Boss*. New York: Bloomsbury, 2012.

Antos, Jason D. *Shea Stadium*. Charleston, S.C.: Arcadia, 2007.

Berkow, Ira. *Summers at Shea*. Chicago: Triumph, 2013.

Bernstein, Sid, with Arthur Aaron. *It's Sid Bernstein Calling*. New York: Jonathan David, 2002.

Blomberg, Ron, with Dan Schlossberg. *Designated Hebrew: The Ron Blomberg Story*. New York: Sports Publishing, 2006.

Cannon, James, and Scott Cannon. *Gerald R. Ford: An Honorable Life*. Ann Arbor: University of Michigan Press, 2013.

Caro, Robert A. *The Power Broker: Robert Moses and the Fall of New York*. New York: Knopf, 1974.

Cohen, Robert W. *The Lean Years of the Yankees, 1965-1975*. New York: McFarland, 2004.

Droleskey, Thomas. *Meeting the Mets: A Quirky History of a Quirky Team*. Thomas A. Droleskey, 2012.

Eskenazi, Gerald. *Gang Green*. New York: Simon & Schuster, 1998.

Firestone, Bernard J., and Alexej Ugrinsky. *Gerald Ford and the Politics of Post-Watergate America*. Westport, Conn.: Greenwood Press, 1993.

Fischler, Stan. *The Triumphant Islanders: Hockey's New Dynasty*. New York: Dodd Mead, 1976.

Gallagher, Mark. *The Yankee Encyclopedia*. New York: Sports Publishing, 2003.

Gershman, Michael. *Diamonds: The Evolution of the Ballpark*. New York: Houghton Mifflin, 1993.

Golenbock, Peter. *George: The Poor Little Rich Boy Who Built the Yankee Empire*. New York: Wiley, 2009.

Madden, Bill. *Steinbrenner: The Last Lion of Baseball*. New York: HarperCollins, 2010.

McCann, Joseph T. *Terrorism on American Soil: A Concise History of Plots and Perpetrators from the Famous to the Forgotten*. Boulder, Colo.: Sentient Publications, 2006.

Rose, Howie, and Phil Pepe. *Put It In the Book!: A Half-Century of Mets Mania*. New York: Triumph, 2013.

Shapiro, Michael. *Bottom of the Ninth: Branch Rickey, Casey Stengel, and the Daring Scheme to Save Baseball From Itself*. New York: Times Books, 2009.

Smith, Curt. *Storied Stadiums*. New York: Carroll & Graf, 2001.

Torre, Joe, and Tom Verducci. *The Yankee Years*. New York: First Anchor Books, 2010.

Trumpbour, Robert C. *The New Cathedrals: Politics and Media in the History of Stadium Construction*. Syracuse: Syracuse University Press, 2007.

Zachter, Mort. *Gil Hodges: A Hall of Fame Life*. Lincoln: University of Nebraska Press, 2015.

Websites

appelpr.com, baseballlibrary.com, baseball-almanac.com, baseball-reference.com, centerfieldmaz.com, football-reference.com, grantland.com, qgazzette.com, loge13.com, mets.com, mets360.com, newstimes.com, newyorkjets.com, newyorktimes.com, *New York Times* online archive, njjewishnews.com, nydailynews.com, nypost.com, nywf64.com, proskatinghisoricalfoundation.org, sabr.org, sportsonearth.com, thebeatles.com, thenation.com, ultimateclassicrock.com, wikipedia.com, and youtube.com.

Magazines/Publications/Videos

Baseball Digest, April 1975; Giants Official Media Guide, 1975; *Jet*, November 13, 1975; Jets Official Media Guide, 1975; Last Play at Shea, 2010 Documentary; Mets Official Game Program, 1975; Mets Official Media Guide, 1975; Mets Official Yearbook, 1975; Mets 1975 Video Yearbook (SNY); NBC News, June 1975; *Sport*, November 1975; *Street and Smith's Baseball*, 1970; WNBC-TV Sports Report, April 1975; Yankees Official Game Program, 1975; and Yankees Official Media Guide, 1975.

Index

A

Acosta, Hon. Rolando T., 64–66

Agee, Tommie, 128

Anderson, Dave, 63–64, 76

Appel, Marty, 133–135, 148, 156

Arbour, Al, 106

B

Baldwin, Rick, 91

Barkum, Jerome, 119

Beame, Mayor Abraham, 11, 96

Beatles, The, 13, 54–58, 62, 112, 155

Bernstein, Sid, 55

Berra, Yogi, 5, 8, 40, 75, 80, 83, 85–88, 155

Bladt, Rick, 42

Blomberg, Ron, 18–19, 22, 27–28, 36

Bonds, Bobby, 25–26, 31, 37, 41, 76, 83

Brinkman, Ed, 36, 42

Bunning, Jim, 62

Burke, Michael, 6, 38–39

C

Carey, Hugh, 96

Carlin, George, 102–103

Carlton, Steve, 77–78, 89

Caro, Robert A., 15, 149

Carter, Gary, 88, 145, 146

Caster, Richard, 115, 118, 120–123, 142–143

Chambliss, Chris, 42

Chase, Chevy, 102, 103

Church, Ryan, 154

Citi Field, ix, 150–151, 154, 156

Clapton, Eric, 57

Clash, The, 57

Coggins, Rich, 42

Columbia University, 65

Cone, David, 153

Continental Baseball League, 51–53

Creedence Clearwater Revival, 57

Cronin, Joe, 18

Crosley, Powel, 49

Cuyahoga Wrecking Company, 5

Cy Young Award, 14, 24, 26, 41, 71–72, 77, 78, 139

D

Davis, Miles, 57

Davis, Steve, 118

Deacon, Bill, x

Dempsey, Rick, 42–43

Devine, Bing, 49

DeWitt Clinton High School, 64

DiMaggio, Joe, 17, 40, 70, 89

Durso, Joseph, 45, 86

E

Ebbets Field, 4, 95, 135, 143

Emperor Hirohito, 14, 118–119

Erving, Julius, 109, 110, 115

F

Figueroa, Ed, 41

Finley, Charles O., 18, 24

Flanagan, Mike, 42

Flynn, Pete, ix–x, xii, 13–15, 58–60, 116

Ford, Gerald, 2, 96, 98–100, 113, 118

Ford, Whitey, 5, 40

Fraunces Tavern, 100, 101

Frazier, Walt, 108

Fromme, Lynette "Squeaky," 98

G

Gantt, Greg, 116

Garelik, Sanford, 30

Garrett, Carl, 118

Gentry, Gary, 62

Gerosa, Lawrence, 53

Giants Stadium, 111, 116, 129, 136, 144

Giles, Warren C., 48

Gooden, Dwight, 145, 153

Graham, Rev. Billy, 61

Grambling College, 127–128, 137

Grand Funk Railroad, 11, 57

Grant, M. Donald, 30, 60, 85, 87, 88, 139

H

Harrelson, Bud, 21, 84, 146–147, 155

Heckscher, August, 13

Hodges, Gil, 84–85, 92

Houk, Ralph, 18

Humble Pie, 57

Hunt, Ron, 70

Hunter, Jim "Catfish," 24–31, 37, 41, 76, 77, 78, 83, 106, 119

I

Ice Capades, 61
Iselin, Philip, 12, 119

J

James Monroe High School, 91
Jaws, 104
Jennings, Dave, 116
Jethro Tull, 57
Joel, Billy, 57–58
John, Elton, 57, 112
Johnson, Davey, 75, 145
Jones, Cleon, 75, 83–85, 87, 145,
   151
Joplin, Janis, 57

K

Kapstein, Jerry, 24
Kiner, Ralph, 89
King, Billie Jean, 111, 112
Kingman, Dave, 76, 80–81, 83,
   97, 139, 140
Koosman, Jerry, 59, 64, 72,
   74–75, 76, 78–79, 83, 86, 88,
   91, 138–139, 140, 147–148
Kranepool, Ed, 7, 9, 59, 70, 78,
   90, 91–92, 138, 155

L

LaGuardia Airport, 22, 62, 101,
   116, 128, 143
Landers, Barry, 32
Lennon, John, 112–113

Lewis, Freddie, 110
Lockwood, Skip, 93
Lolich, Mickey, 27, 81
Lyle, Sparky, 25

M

Maddox, Elliott, 23, 31, 33–37
Madison Square Garden, 39, 55,
   105, 109
Madlock, Bill, 78, 93
Mara, John, 10, 11, 128, 129,
   131
Mara, Wellington, 10, 11, 102,
   136
Marion, Marty, 52
Martin, Billy, 40–42, 83
Martin, George, 56
Matlack, Jon, 13, 64, 78–79, 81,
   83, 86, 88, 139–140
Mauch, Gene, 87
May, Rudy, 83
Mays, Willie, 26, 89
McCartney, Paul, 57, 58
McGraw, Tug, 80, 140–141
Melchionni, Bill, 110
Millan, Felix, 67–69, 85, 86
Miller, Dyar, 42
Monroe, Earl, 108
Moore, Sarah Jane, 68, 99
Morton, Craig, 103, 116,
   129–130
Moses, Robert, 3–4, 15, 64, 149,
   151

Munson, Thurman, 31, 42, 98
Murcer, Bobby, 8–9, 25–26
Murtaugh, Danny, 47

N
Namath, Joe, 9, 13, 63, 116–124, 127, 129, 143–144
Nastase, Ilie, 111
Nelson, Lindsay, 62, 63, 141
Nixon, Richard, 86, 96–97, 113–114, 152

O
O'Malley, Walter, 3, 53

P
Paley, William S., 39
Payson, Joan Whitney, 89, 91, 141–142
Pelé, 60, 111
Polo Grounds, 4, 30, 48, 53, 58, 69–70, 134, 151
Pope John Paul II, 62

R
Reed, Willis, 108
Resch, Chico, 106–108
Reuschel, Rick, 92, 93
Rickey, Branch, 51–53
Riggins, John, 1–2, 115, 118, 124, 142
Rivers, Mickey, 41
Robinson, Eddie, 127, 137

Rolling Stones, The, 57
Rose, Howie, 6–7, 15, 32, 55, 72, 74, 137, 154, 155
Rumsfeld, Donald, 96

S
Saturday Night Live, 102
Seaver, Tom, 8, 13, 45, 57, 59, 64, 70–72, 74, 76–79, 83, 86, 88, 92–93, 97, 139, 140, 146, 155
Seitz, Peter, 24
Shea, William, 4, 149–151
Sheppard, Bob, 40
Simon, Paul, 57
Simon and Garfunkel, 57
Smith, Red, 87
Smith, Stan, 111
Springsteen, Bruce, 57, 115
Stargell, Willie, 47
Staub, Rusty, 76, 81.97, 155
Staubach, Roger, 103, 130, 140
Steinbrenner, George, 6, 9, 18, 19, 34, 37, 38, 39, 40–41, 83, 125
Stengel, Casey, 47, 70, 88–89, 141
Stern, Carl, 96, 97
Sting, 54, 56, 57
Stottlemyre, Mel, 19, 22, 27
Strawberry, Darryl, 145, 152, 153
Sugar, Bert, 5, 135

T
Tate, Randy, 87–88, 92
The Who, 57
Tiant, Luis, 28
Torre, Joe, 62, 67–69, 76, 78,
    138, 153
Tottenville High School, 64

U
Unser, Del, 68, 76.97
Ure, Midge, xi, xii

V
Vail, Mike, 97
Velez, Otto, 42
Virdon, Bill, 8, 17–19, 23–24,
    25, 37–38, 40, 41, 82, 83

W
Wagner, Mayor Robert, 3, 4, 47,
    48–49, 51, 53
Watergate Office Complex, 96,
    113

Weaver, Earl, 42
Westmoreland, General
    William, 32
White, Randy, 129
White, Roy, 42
Whitfield, Terry, 42
Williams, Dick, 18
Williams, Doug, 127–128, 137
Wilson, Mookie, 146, 147
World Football League, 123, 129

Y
Yale Bowl, 10–11, 102, 125, 128,
    129
Yankee Stadium (1), 5–6, 8, 10,
    17, 19, 21–22, 25, 28, 30, 36,
    38–39, 65, 127, 111, 129,
    133–134
Yankee Stadium (2), 135,
    143–144, 152
Yastrzemski, Carl, 79